PRODUCT BRANDING MARKETING

DISCOVER THE SUPER 5 PART

PRODUCT BRANDING MARKETING

PLAN THAT BUILDS A STRONG

PRODUCT BRAND CONSUMERS

LOVE AND WORSHIP

BY TANIA MARIE SHELDON

Tania Marie Sheldon

PUBLISHED BY BURSTBOOKS

Unit 12 /30 Upper Queen St Auckland, New Zealand 1010.

www.BurstBooks.biz

Cover by Gareth Thomas.

For information about special discounts available for bulk purchases, sales promotions, fund-raising and educational needs, contact BurstBooks at publisher@BurstBooks.biz

BurstBooks.biz

TABLE OF CONTENTS

CHAPTER ONE

SUMMARY

Your brand represents everything that people experience to do with your company. Your Brand is working for you 24 hours a day seven days a week. Influencing the thoughts and behavior of everybody interacting with that brand. Customers and employees have an impression of the brand based upon their experience. You alone, as the visionary, have a future vision of the brand as you want it to be.

WHAT IS A BRAND?

Most companies put some kind of branding into place. Many also have an accidental and unintended brand. If you don't know the difference, then you're branding by accident. A logo is not your brand. A logo is a visual representation of your brand and logos are part of a science called semiotics. The logo is a visual trigger that represents your entire brand.

Tania Marie Sheldon

A brand is something psychological. It's a meme or mental energy. It's what all your customers and employees and everybody else think of your company. We are dealing with psychology. It's when all the interactions, conversations and activities come together. That is what your brand is.

I said some people brand by design and others by accident. As the founder of your company, you can see it in all its glory, the brand as you believe it should be. You are the visionary of the brand and its creator. That makes you the brand leader. Customers and employees have an impression of the brand based upon their experience. You alone as the visionary have a future vision of the brand as you want it to be. As the brand leader, you're the only person that's going to do that. The logo is a metaphor of the brand that you envision when people see that logo that captures your energy.

This forms an emotional connection to people so you can rally them behind your vision. We know that branding got its name from a hot iron used on cattle. But branding is far more than visual design and graphics. It's an emotional and psychological paradigm. There is a lot of science backing it up and a lot of data that you can use in developing a strong and effective brand.

Your brand represents everything that people experience to do with your company. It is working for you 24 hours a day seven days a week. Influencing the thoughts and behavior of everybody interacting with that brand. The brand is a potent business tool. it's the personality or persona of your business. A personification is an excellent way to describe it. That brand has to make you more attractive to customers, and it has to make them like you. It has to convey who you are, what you do, how you do it and why you do it.

Your brand has a visual identity. That includes your logo, website, literature, formatting and packaging. It includes your name and slogan. Who you are, is usually what customers first come across when interacting with your brand. It needs to explain to them the benefits of interacting with your brand. So it needs to communicate the values of your business. What drives your business? What behavior they can expect, what about you and your business inspires trust?

CHAPTER TWO

SUMMARY

The American Marketing Association describes the elements of a brand as the following:

- name
- term
- visible sign
- symbolic device
- design

You use it to differentiate your business from others.

Your brand must resonate with your clients whenever they enter into contact. Every time they touch your brand or connect to some of these interactions. Consider the last time a business impressed you. Today's commercial world is callous and competitive. Much more so than before. Your brand can do one of three things. It can grow, it can engage, or it can perish.

Great brands deliver the message and are very clear about it. You need to be concise and clear when presenting your brand to consumers. They need to know very well what it is that you do and exactly how it benefits them. Your brand makes a guarantee to your customers. It makes a promise which is a lot more important than a logo design or some catchphrase on your brochure. Or some billboard with advertising shown on it.

Many companies nowadays are cunning about social media. Social media is effective in enhancing your marketing. It's ideal for lead generation, and those leads can become your customers. Today the consumers are in charge, and they don't have to check out your social media channels. Internet marketing represents an enormous opportunity.

You need to get the right mixture of media to reach your goals, and that requires a great deal of testing. Usually, there are several ways to reach the individuals that you want. You will need to look for the way that is most beneficial to get your message right for the consumer. Then you will need to ensure that you're providing them with the right message.

There are so many choices of marketing media nowadays, TV, radio et cetera. People want to use iPods and smartphones. They are always on Facebook or some other social media site like Twitter. They don't spend much time with traditional media.

POSITIONING YOUR BRAND FOR SUCCESS

First up I want to explain to you what a brand is. People are often confused about, so I want you to think about some of the most popular brands in the world. Think about large famous brands and what they stand for.

I'd like you to think about Disney. That's one of the biggest brands in the world, and everyone knows what they stand for. From the chief executive officer down to the point of sale staff. Everybody knows what their company brand is and they all know what it stands for. It's a heck of a lot more than a logo it's more than any advertising material. To understand your brand you have to understand your customers. The psychology of their wants and needs.

Your brand has to resonate with the customers whenever they come into contact. Whenever they touch your company or interact with some of its elements. Whenever those customers have anything to do with your company. You have to understand their needs and wants it's imperative that you remember that. The most proactive company is the one that wins the customers over.

Your brand makes a promise to your customers. This is far more important than a logo or some slogan on your brochure or some sign with advertising on it. It's everything involved with their experience of your company. It's the promise that your employees understand. The commitment you make to your customers and to the media and the public. Think about the last time you got blown away by a company think about the last time a company impressed you. Or the last time a company disappointed or annoyed you.

It's all about the brand. If you have a bad experience in a store with a rude salesperson that will define your brand experience. Compare the impact of that to the logo. Somebody that has that experiences will tell their friends and workmates. They're going to tell more people that they had a bad experience than if they had had a good one.

If you don't develop, you're going to die. You must always keep your customers engaged. You must strive to make improvements in your communications and interactions with customers.

Always be clear in the delivery of your message. Credibility and trust are critical. A satisfied customer becomes a loyal customer, and you do need to follow through. I did once see a quote from the CEO at Virgin Atlantic. He said at the end of the day, we all fly to the same places as everybody else. We keep our customers on the plane happy. We take care of them so they're going to keep coming back, buying our product, so branding is a huge marketing tool.

When people are on a flight on the plane one of the last things they do is text to a friend or message on Facebook. If they end up telling them what a positive experience they had it adds to the interaction with your brand. You must create a pleasant and happy atmosphere for your customers. Every time they interact with your brand.

Tania Marie Sheldon

Social media is beneficial in lead generation. Those leads can become customers. You can communicate with customers and encourage them to make more purchases. You can help them to make referrals and bring in new customers. You can influence them using push marketing. Today the customers are in control. They don't have to follow your social media channels. This has changed from the past. In the past 30 years ago, they had to listen to what was on TV, or on the radio. You can put out your message and get customers.

In the past there was no real communication taking place. Back then people would do business with you because they had no other choice. There was a different kind of entrepreneurialism taking place. Today there are far more opportunities. You do have to work harder at getting customers because of the competition. You have to have better marketing systems. You have to take better care of your customers so that they will bring in more business referrals. You want them talking about you on social media. Telling all their friends on blogs and Facebook, and all the other avenues and social media. Unfortunately, that means they can say bad things about you too.

If they had a bad experience with you, they are going to tell people about that, and this can hurt your brand. That's why you have to make sure you keep your customers happy. You have to make sure that when they leave, it was a good experience.

I know a lot of people think about marketing but are not doing it in a real way. They think they don't have enough time to put into it. There are some common mistakes that people make, and it is time-consuming. It can also be costly but what matters most is the ROI. It stands for return on investment. Many people have no way to tell if their marketing is working. This can be very frustrating and can waste a great deal of money.

It all comes down to tracking which is a critical element of marketing. Online marketing has a massive advantage in this respect. There are many different ways to track your marketing. Google analytics and the Facebook pixel being the biggest players. On Facebook, you can perform acurate customer demographic targeting. You can get down into some very detailed features. Age, where they live, what books they read and what interests they have. When they have had children and the age of those children. All sorts of things and it's astounding what you can find out. That all exists for you to use as a marketer.

Online marketing represents a huge opportunity. Marketing is crucial to your business and without it, your business can't operate. You have to understand the target market you have to know who they are. I'm not talking about identifying a person. Rather a persona that represents the majority of your customers. With tools like Facebook, this becomes much easier. You can also do surveys using SurveyMonkey. Surveys are a popular marketing tool for research. Using surveys you can find some information that Facebook doesn't provide. Quite often when using a survey, you have to incentivize that to encourage people to fill the survey out.

They can win a camera or a trip overseas or something to that nature. You have to consider why a customer would do business with you. Once you understand that you can get the right message through to your customers. You also have to choose the right media for communication with those customers.

There is a vast number of ways you can advertise today. You can use traditional media, radio, TV, billboards, and direct mail. You can do social media. There are so many different options; there is no single one that's perfect. In fact, it's good that there are so many to try and you can do them all. You need to find the right mix of media to be successful. That takes a lot of testing. Usually there are two or three types that reach the people that you want.

Before Internet marketing people used different forms of tracking. With direct mail, for example, you can ask them to call through to an 800 number. Today you can get them to go to a website or Facebook. You can use the Facebook pixel and other methods to track your customers. Also, a social media campaign might work better in one month than it does in another. You won't know unless you test. You have to be trying all sorts of things and testing them all to make sure that your branding is effective.

Once you know what works, you can tie it in with your media relations. You should have plans for your company, a corporate goal. You might have a three year, a five year, a ten-year plan. That plan has to match your organizational goals.

These plans have to be flexible even though it often takes months to develop them. You never know when something will change. New competitors come into the marketplace and take customers away. New customers and markets make themselves available. You have to be re-evaluating all the time. Your objectives have to be evident once you got your plan put together; you have to target your customers.

You can't be all things to all people, and you have to have a narrow section of customers that you have focused onto. That's your customer base. They are the ones most likely to buy your products and services and give you the best return on investment. They are the ones that match your customer avatar and your customer demographic.

Your customer avatars should represent your primary demographic. We also have a secondary demographic but you had best to narrow your focus to the primary. You can't be all things to all people. You have to target the primary demographic. Target the most effective social media outlets for the demographic. Once you've got an idea of what your demographic is you can survey them. Ether online or in focus groups to get a better understanding of the thought processes.

Many business people are very busy and if you try to get hold of them on the phone you get stuck on voicemail. They don't answer. For people like that, it might be more useful to send direct mail and email. Many wouldn't even look at a direct mail letter. It might go in the bin or sit on the desk. They may have an emplyee that checks their mail. There are so many variables involved, and you don't want to concern yourself with them all. Your approach is to find the most effective media outlet through testing. Not fathoming out the reason why for individual customers. Through using surveys, you can figure out the best way to contact them.

Many people don't understand that advertising is a statistical numbers game. They may try something once and see that it didn't work and decide that it never will. Things take time and often take many efforts. Direct mail may take several attempts and results may trickle in. With direct mail you can try different things. Different colored papers, and different envelopes. Some of these things will get better results than others; you need to test the medium. Once you have the best means of delivering your message you can start testing the results.

Always remember that return on investment. You have to measure the results from everything and determine what is useful. You have to measure your advertising because otherwise you're sitting in the dark. You can't be lazy about this particular point.

Many media channels can apply for every instance of marketing. You have to apply the appropriate media to the circumstances. So you may have a personal preference for social media, direct mail or something like that. You can't allow that to prejudice your marketing decision. Test and verify everything with ROI in mind.

Conversation with customers can give you some idea of their preferred media. You can ask them if you wish. This can make you and your marketing efforts more productive. Determine the way that is best to get your message to the customer. Then make sure that you're giving them the right message. Target the message. It has to be consistent with your branding. You have to provide them with an offer. Let them know what you want them to do otherwise you're wasting your time and money.

Nikkei has a tagline "just do it." That's been around for years, and they keep using it. They found something that works for them and kept it. You need to find what works for you and the personality of your brand. Take a look at your company's personality, that's persona and that of your customers. You are trying to see how these two can communicate with each other. Take a look at the qualities of your persona and list them. All your communication needs to match up with this persona.

If you get this right that all your communications and messages will be on target and optimized. It doesn't matter if it's a picture a slogan or some other means of communication. You have to keep it brief. Keep it concise because you don't know how much time the customer has paid attention to your message. Often they only look at for a short time. For them it's something trivial. If someone is driving to another city and they go past a billboard. What's the point of 10 lines of text when they've only got five seconds to look at it. It would be better off with some representative image and a brief slogan. You have to make sure that the message is right for the time and place as well as the specific customer.

Traditional media is perfect for the news. People trust it for news and weather. Each type of media has its pros and cons, but you have to look at it from the customer point of view, not from yours. Publicity is a form of free advertising. Social media takes it to a whole new level, and it can be either good or bad for you.

One of the best examples of branding today, personal branding, is president Trump. He used to be in real estate where he spent a lot of money, and he made a lot of money. He also lost a lot, but one thing for sure that Trump learned was the value of branding. Trump has made a lot of money off his brand, and he has lent it to other companies. There were even trump steaks. So he knows all about branding. Trumps brand on social media is worth over $250 million. He is all over the place. Trump makes mistakes on his twitter and social media goes crazy. Somehow for him, that seems to strengthen the brand even more.

Keep Trumps battles in mind when you deal with the media yourself. Keep in mind how he puts his foot and his mouth because you may not be as lucky as Trump. You may not be the Teflon Don when it comes to abusing your brand values. That's because your brand is not so strong in the first place. Don't give the media the wrong pitch or a story that is not right. You have to have a good relationship with the particular media and the people in it. Don't waste their time with the wrong stories. They don't want any content that is not beneficial to them.

You will be dealing with many different forms of media. Including newspapers and press people. You have to know how to communicate with them and give them what they want. It's okay to ask. Rather than waste time, publicity is something that you should outsource if you're not good at it.

Social media has a great deal of value, but it can also be a time waster. You need to get onto Twitter, and you need to have a game plan. You need to have a strategy; otherwise, social media can be dangerous. Many companies get onto social media then present themselves as a person rather than a brand. This is a big mistake. Your profile needs to represent your company or your brand.

The great thing about Facebook is that you can target the demographic of your customers. LinkedIn is pretty much the same. LinkedIn is for a different market altogether, being business oriented. LinkedIn can be a beneficial media avenue for business to business communications. It's a great place to project your brand in a professional sense.

You can also learn a great deal about individual customers. Details about customer persona. This can be a great help with planning. So there are plenty of opportunities that spring from social media. Social media is a massive business. There are plenty of people that are experts on social media that can help you with your business.

You have to deliver wow to your customers, or they won't want to do business with you at all. You have to communicate with them. You have to show them that you care about them and that you understand. You have to invest in a solid marketing strategy. Not a half-hearted approach.

Consistency is crucial to a strong brand. You have to understand how the image looks from the outside. All the promotional materials and advertising have to be cohesive and consistent. This is what forms an impression in the minds of the customers. If they like what they see, they'll buy from you, and if they don't, they will spread the word that you are no good.

There are companies out there that are a big mess. They have chaotic offices and no real goals in the business as they exist in the present moment. It doesn't matter how good your sales are today. You have to have a direction to get your business out there to the customers and keep going in the future. Every company has weaknesses and can strive to improve and do better. The business environment changes and the brand has to adapt and change as well.

Assess your brand and your customer's responses to it. Many companies start with an edge in the market and end up with many competitors. Under those circumstances, your brand has to adapt, or you will not be competitive. The customers themselves can change. So you have to keep the conversation going and keep analyzing your customer avatar.

Ask your customers how they feel when they do business with you. Watch their social media and blogs to see what's said about your company. What things do they often talk about? Look up your competition and look for new opportunities that come up. You have to react when the opportunities come. Sometimes online the window only lasts for six months before its too late.

If you can't do the things yourself what you have to do is hire professionals to help you do these tasks. Find the best people in the business and leverage their skills. Consider it an investment in your business's long-term success and growth. Keep tracking and measuring everything. Get your top management staff together and talk to them about marketing. Talk to them about your brand and how to strengthen it.

You need to spend about 30% of your budget at most on marketing. Especially in the first three years of starting the business. Once you've established a known brand you can spend less such as 7%. This could be 5 to 10 years down the track.

It also depends on your competition and your market. Most of the large brands have been very aggressive and spent a lot of money in getting to where they are. They've hired the best people at great expense. You're going to have to do the same at the beginning if you want to have a strong brand. You'll have to do the work and spend the money. You can model off those successful brands. Look at what they do and how they do it. If you make some sacrifice there's nothing to stop you from doing the same.

CHAPTER THREE

SUMMARY

All organizations have customers. Be it a commercial profit-making firm or a nonprofit charity. Marketing is all about creating that relevance in the mind of the customer. Doing it in a better way than your competition. It's also a case of confronting constant change. Changes and marketplaces. Changes and customers mindset due to demographics and consumer trends. The marketing side of your business should be a central hub of the wheel. The wheel represents all the other activities of your company.

Most written marketing plans include an executive summary. That gives an overview of the plan. The situation analysis that could be a swot analysis of your company. The market opportunity, the competition, and the customer. For consumers, emotional benefits are the most important. For companies, it's the economic and financial factors. There is usually a different type of person involved in the purchasing process too. Segmenting your customers allows your marketing to be more efficient. You can segment the market targeting upon income level, age, gender, and other factors. Segmentation tells us how we will appeal to customers. It helps to narrow down your audience to a select group. Your marketing message won't appeal to everyone, so this is the best approach.

Positioning happens in the mind of the consumer. How you position your product in the market will determine its success. Finally your strategy, you must create goals towards your financial objectives. The goals should also be relevant to your marketing strategy. They should be time allocated which adds to their accuracy.

BRANDING & MARKETING

All organizations have customers. Be it a commercial profit-making firm or a nonprofit charity. To survive those organizations have to be relevant to their customers. Marketing is all about creating that relevance in the mind of the customer. Doing it in a better way than your competition.

If you're smart you will see marketing as an investment in your company. It may well be the most critical function in your company. That's how companies wage competitive warfare with each other. Those companies that don't wage this war don't last long in business. Because there is always competition. It's also a case of confronting constant change. Changes in marketplaces. Changes in customer's mindset due to demographics and consumer trends.

As a marketer, you have to adapt to all this. New competitors entering the marketplace, and older competitors making adaptations, steal your customers. There are also economic conditions to contend with. Innovations and technology, things like social media that impact on marketing. Even things like government regulations have a significant impact on consumer behavior.

Sometimes you can predict these things but often you can't. In either case, you have to adapt to them. A well-planned marketing strategy and a documented marketing plan can be a big help. A marketing strategy defines your target customers. It provides you with information on that demographic. The marketing strategy defines how you will engage with those people. The marketing plan defines steps that you will take to put in place the marketing strategy.

The marketing side of your business should be a central hub of the wheel. The wheel represents all the other activities in your company. The marketing part of your business should be coordinating all the other activities. To create value for the customer. As marketing is central to the business, branding is central to marketing. You want to have a strong brand and experienced marketing staff. The most successful companies in the world invest in branding. Their marketing operations depend upon it.

Marketing planning has four-phases, analysis, strategy, tactical and measurement. In the initial planning stage, you learn about your customers. You want to know how and why they buy your product or service. You also analyze the competition and compare them using a swot test or similar. At this stage you will also need to analyze the market itself. Its potential for the most attractive return on investment.

Marketing Planning

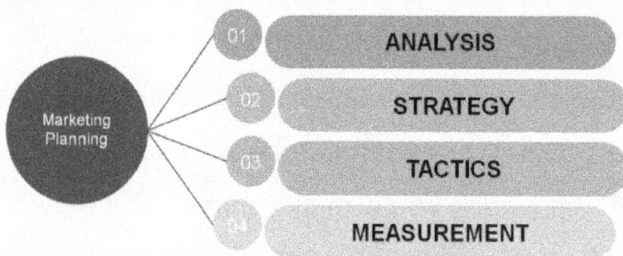

During the strategic phase, you use information from the planning phase. Determine how you will position your products and services in the market. In the tactical phase you have to create your actual marketing programs. Use them to execute the strategy around your products and services. You will also be setting prices and creating sales material and marketing communications.

During the measurement phase, you analyze data and feedback from your marketing operations. Determine the effect of your efforts to date. You need to find out if you've targeted the right demographic. If that demographic is behaving in the way that you anticipated. The measurement phase helps you determine your return on investment. ROI is the most important thing.

The planning phase takes a lot of work, but it's the most critical part. It takes a lot of discipline to complete a proper planning phase. It requires a skilled team to develop and execute a marketing strategy. This can include both internal and external partners. Like media agencies and advertising firms.

You need to have a multi-skilled team helping and your marketing enterprise. This will include a finance team that determines your budget. This team may also include an accountant. Their job is to cut your losses and maximize your return on investment. They also may assist in obtaining capital and financial loans.

You also need marketing researchers in your team. This team will determine the needs of your customer. They will test new product ideas and different advertising strategies. This marketing research applies throughout the entire marketing process.

The technical team develops your products and services. Often today they are programmers. They may be engineers or scientists doing research and development. It depends what you're actual business is. This team needs to know what products are appropriate for your target market. Also what the needs are of that market.

The design team is often a separate department in many companies. They try to give your customers a rewarding experience to enhance the brand promise. Many organizations have a sales team. They will work with the marketing department. They are more or less the frontline troops at the point of sale.

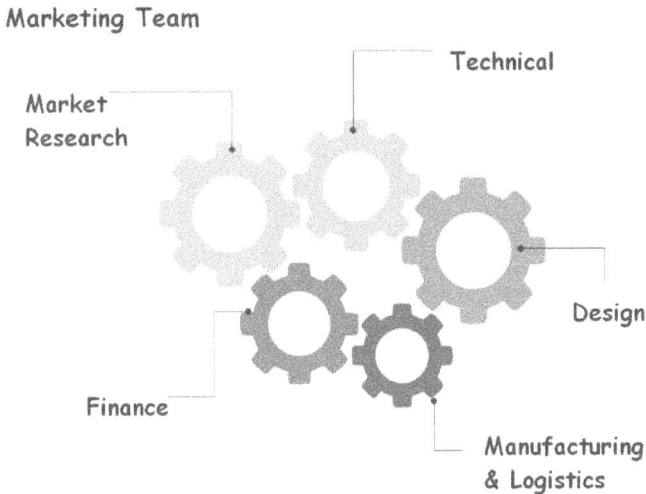

Marketing Team

Market Research

Technical

Design

Finance

Manufacturing & Logistics

Depending on your business you may want manufacturing and operations, people, even logistics. These are the manufacturers and delivery people. You may have a customer support team, or you may outsource it. There may be public relations and even a marketing consultant.

These different people make up your team. They are the key players. They need to know their role when it comes to developing a marketing strategy for your business. They need to be able to work together to that goal. One way to make this happen is with a formal written marketing plan. It document the planning process. It will include information that the team has learned about the market. This includes competition and customers. This is critical information. It will be the basis for the strategies that your team determines. It also helps to align the team.

A well-written plan is essential to create presentations and training programs. It will give direction to external partners. You will make heavy use of this plan, so you better get it right. Scheduling and budgeting can also derive from the marketing plan.

Most written marketing plans include the following. An executive summary that gives an overview of the plan. The situation analysis that could be a swot analysis of your company. The market opportunity, the competition, and the customer. There should be a strategy section. That outlines your market segmentation describing who you are targeting. Tt will also describe your product positioning within the market. The tactical programs defining products and prices, promotion and distribution. There should be a financial section. That outlines the return on investment projections and budget requirements. Finally, an implementation plan with the timetable that outlines who handles what.

Marketing Planning Process

01 ANALYSIS		Target Persona?
02 STRATEGY		Positioning?
03 TACTICS		Execution?
04 MEASUREMENT		Feedback?

Write the plan throughout the entire planning process rather than leaving it to the end. You can do it in an agile fashion and update the plan as you go. Agile is a great concept to apply to a marketing plan as it is dynamic and changes with conditions in the market. Such a program will help you stay ahead of your competition.

You will have heard of business to business, and business to customer, you need to know the difference. The marketing planning process is the same for both, how you do certain things, in either case, will vary. People buy products and services for several benefits. These benifits are functional, economic and emotional. B2B and B2C differ in the balance between these three things.

For consumers, emotional benefits are the most important. For companies, it's the economic and financial factors. There is usually a different type of person involved in the purchasing process too. Companies are more analytical and logical when making a buying decision. Consumers are usually buy products for themselves or friends and family. There a lot of emotion involved. Even though there may be some rational decision-making also. You need to understand this to make an obvious and effective marketing strategy. You also need to define it.

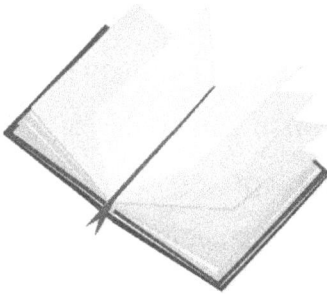

AGILE
Marketing Plan

Choice of market has a significant influence on the size of your consumer base. Define your core business around a primary market benefit. As opportunities increase so do challenges which are not always a good thing. It can bring more competition and means you have to be good at more things.

You may decide to focus on things that your company can already do very well to make consumers happy. You need to define your core business. You also need to define your core competencies and skills. You should not try and do things that you're not skilled at. Your marketing plan can target specific products or services. It canalso target everything that you've got to offer. You can have more than one marketing plan, with an umbrella plan covering all the segmented ones.

Decide hese things before you start the planning process. When marketing a single product target all resources to that products customers. Target all your communications, pricing and everything else. Sometimes it's better to make your marketing strategy around a family of products. This is more efficient for money spent.

You don't make this decision, the consumer does. We always want to put the consumer's perspective first. Your identity in the customer's mind your brand. Regardless of what kind of marketing you're doing. The brand is what the consumers percieve. Decision-making must be from the consumer's perspective. The brand is the promise that you make to your customer about the benefits you can deliver.

If all your products fall under one brand, it makes sense to have a single marketing plan for all those products. That's how the consumer sees it. If you have segmented branding then you can segment your marketing plan. Often consumers won't even know if you have an umbrella company that owns many brands. They will identify the brands that appeal to them. They won't know that you own a family of brands.

Marketing would be a cakewalk if there were no competition. Your competition wants the same thing that you do. You need to understand your competition. You need to know which competitors to focus on and which ones to avoid. You don't want to attack a competitor that's stronger than you. You need to consider your competition throughout your planning process.

You need to look at the critical resources of your competitors. Determine how they get and keep customers. How you do this analysis depends what industry you are in. In technology, you would be looking at research and development. Spending, the number of engineers they use and how many new products they released each year. How they train staff. How the customer service rates. These are common things throughout most industries.

What you do is you create a competitor matrix. It's imperative only to use public information in this matrix. From the matrix you can derive insights to use when deciding on your strategy. If you have a strategy throughout to handle competition you get a large edge in the marketplace. Analyze the features of your products and services compared to the competition. Find which ones perform better and which don't. You can base your marketing strategy upon these benefits to the customer.

Marketing is about acquiring and keeping customers. You have to have an excellent understanding of who they are.

What do they believe in about your products and services and how they will they buy them? You have to have an understanding of what you call a customer. Some companies may have broad definition others may have a narrow one.

If you're selling wallets then a customer is anyone who's going to replace their wallet in the next year. You could define customers around their attitudes and brand preferences. Once you know who your customers are you have to understand their psychology. The mentality about the products and services that you sell. You need a robust customer analysis to develop a solid marketing strategy.

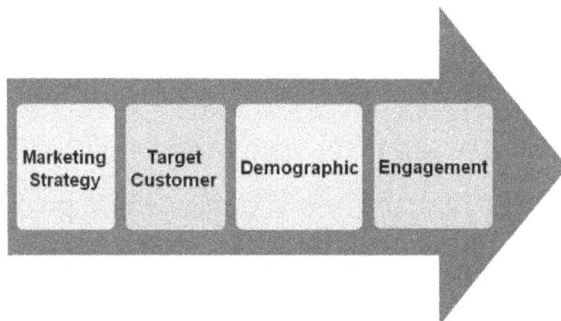

Marketing Strategy	Target Customer	Demographic	Engagement

Customers usually follow a unique set of steps when buying. It could be a split-second decision in a shop. It may be something that takes months like when someone buys a new house or car. The first stage is the need recognition phase. This is when they realize that they need or want something. It's an internal trigger driven by a psychological motive. Like if someone is thirsty and decide to buy a milkshake. If somebody sees an advert for a soft drink and they are not thirsty, then they're not going to buy it anyway. Without the need recognition phase, there is no sale made.

Next is the information search known as ZMOT. This is when consumers go hunting often online for reviews. They seek information about the product to determine if it will fulfill their need. They also compare products to find the best one. In the Internet age, this is much easier for consumers. Marketers can observe and analyze this behavior using tracking . Customers make their decision based upon the features of the product. What they think are the most important and what the brand delivers. Generally, they narrow it down to one brand and one product, that being the best.

The next phase is the sale phase which may take a matter of seconds, or it could take months. Some products need financing and others have a complicated installation process. Usually, more expensive complex products take longer to buy. In the post-purchase phase, consumers use their product and conclude its usefulness. This is with regard to fulfilling their needs. It is at this point that other consumers will seek out their opinion to make their own buying decisions. In this sense, it is a cycle. The post-purchase phase is crucial to marketers. Aat this point consumers can share their experience. Consumers may also have buyers remorse. They regret having spent the money. This is not uncommon, but it tends to pass.

Marketers can capitalize upon this stage. They can emphasize any positive frame of mind. They can also influence the buying decisions of other consumers. Remind the consumer what a great buy it is that they made. This can is sometimes done with customer support. They can also encourage other consumers who are seeking information about products. Getting referrals and reviews as an example.

Good marketers know that they have a role to play in each step of the buying process. It doesn't stop at the initial sale. If you do it right, your customers will be making sales for you.

Consumer Matrix

High

Loyalty

| Only Buy from Competitor | Ready To Buy Only from You |
| Never Buy At All | Ready To Buy Also Competitors |

Low

Willingness

High

When analyzing a market, you can group customers into four types. First up are the ones that are ready to buy. They may already be a customer. They would never buy from your competition and have commitment to your brand. The second group is the same except that they will buy from competitors as well. They respect your brand and like your products but also like those of your competition. The third group buys only from the competition. Never from you. The fourth group don't buy the product at all from anybody.

If you can tap into the fourth group that's a new source of revenue. That is not taken away from competitors. By tapping into this fourth group you are increasing the markets size. You can estimate the number of potential customers in each of these four groups. Then you can decide which group you want to focus on with your marketing strategy. You can learn the number of consumers in each group . You can estimate what percentage of the market you would like to win over to your brand.

Once your analysis is complete, you can start working on the marketing strategy. You should at this point know a lot about your customers and the market. Enough to know where the most potential is to focus your efforts. The first strategy is to segment your market. Break your customers down into homogenous groups.

The next step is targeting where you decide which segments to go after. After this is positioning. This is how you want your customers to see your brand and products versus your competition. You want them to buy yours.

Segmenting your customers allows your marketing to be more efficient. It will enable you to focus on the most relevant customers and waste less money. You can segment the market targeting upon income level, age, gender, and other factors. Demographic targeting is significant for some products and less so for others. Behavioral segmentation looks at the things customers do. It could be the frequency of purchasing online or it could be hobbies and places they like to visit. Finally psychographic segmentation. This is about attitudes and beliefs about the benefits of your product. It might be a need for self-esteem or prestige.

Segmentation tells us how we will appeal to customers. It helps to narrow down your audience to a select group. Your marketing message won't appeal to everyone, so this is the best approach. You want to find that segment that's most inclined to buy your product. Often I look at the demographic data first, and then the behavioral data. I want the most abundant group that will be receptive to my message. Using these tools gives us a strategy for competing. We then can determine what we will say to the market to convince. This is positioning and what we offer them is a value proposition.

Positioning happens in the mind of the consumer. How you position your product in the market will determine its success. The consumer forms opinions about products and services in particular categories. They have perceptions about which products are better or worse. Which contain the features that are more or less important. As a marketer, you can change these beliefs. You can move them around to increase the probability that they will favor your brand. You do this by making a claim and supporting it with credible reasons to buy.

Market Strategy

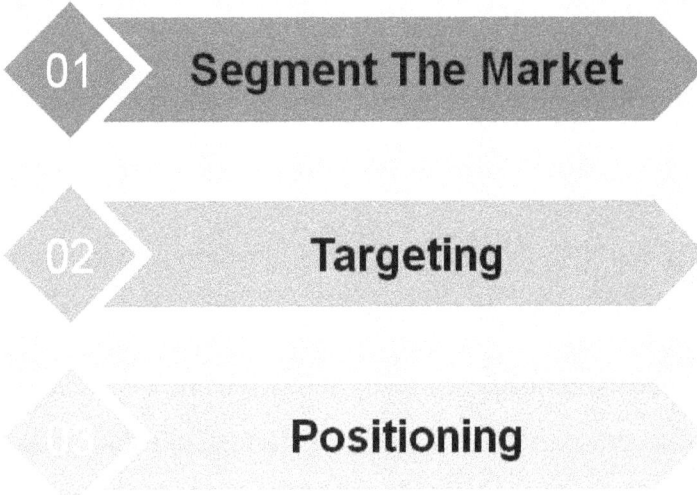

01	Segment The Market

02	Targeting

	Positioning

Look at what your targeted customers are doing today with regards to your product in the market. . What are their current beliefs about the products that are available? What is it that you desire the customers to do, what claims do you make? How do you support those claims and are they authentic?

Finally in the strategy phase you must create goals towards your financial objectives. Goals help you decide what resources to divide and how much. The more aggressive your goals are usually the more resources that will you need. Use Key performance indicators to measure your performance throughout the campaign. Be specific with exact percentages as this makes it more measurable. There is no point in having goals that you can't measure. The goals should also be relevant to your marketing strategy. They should be time allocated which adds to their accuracy.

Now it's time for the tactical marketing program. There are four P's in marketing. Product or service, pricing, promotional communications, and distribution. Distribution is sometimes called "place." So it's product, price, promotion and place. Remember the 4P's of marketing.

Product and service programs refer to how to deliver benefits to the consumer. This includes things like the design, packaging. Also processes involved with dealing with the customer including customer support. It's not only how the product functions but contains the entire consumer experience. It should be consistent with the brand positioning in the brand promise.

Pricing involves setting the price that consumers will pay. The price implies the value that the consumer perceives. Pricing also involves effective communication of that price

Promotion is everything said by the company to the market. It's where you broadcast your value proposition and information about the product. It includes advertising, email, social media, and sales promotion.

Distribution is how the customer gets your product. This is very important to the customer, and the marketing process does not end at the sale. It includes shipping and delivery, service and returns.

The 4P's of marketing work together to convey the value proposition. No single piece is more important than the others. A good marketer uses all the tools available to make the best impression possible. Marketing is all about delivering value to your customers. You do that by offering the right products and services to match the market segment.

You need to get the right product or service for the markets segment. You need to go back to the analysis phase of the planning process. and look at the results of your product analysis. That's where you compare your product features to those of your competition. Look at the customer analysis and market research. Find out what is most important to the customers when they buy. Also look at data on how they perceive your brand and the competition. Your product development team needs guidance on all four of these aspects.

They need to consider what features the product needs. It must compete against the competition and still meet the needs of the customer. You have to emphasize what features are most important to the value proposition. You have to do make it clear what benefits your promising. Don't expect them to know how to do the groundwork, you have to make it clear.

Clarify what benefit you're promising. Then look on the future benefit later and find those features that deliver. Emphasize these when the customer uses the product.

Your development team will need guidance on the performance of these features. Use your value proposition to guide you. How well should the product work in respect to the competition? Again look at your market research and how consumers perceive these features.

The development team will need feedback on the look and feel of the product, what it stands for. Does it express your brand identity? Your development team must understand the product as an entire consumer experience.

It includes everything that the customer comes into contact with both on and offline. The display of the product, how it's packaged, instructions on use. At each point of contact, the consumer will form or reinforce a belief about your brand. If it is consistent, believable and authentic. The more credible it is, the more loyal your customers will become. This is how you build your brand and business.

Test setting prices online in real-time. This is much easier than in a brick and mortar business. Traffic can increased with pay per click advertising. Determine your return on investment can usine scientific statistics. You need to understand the difference between a products cost, price and value. The cost involves all the direct and indirect expenses involved in manufacturing. Price is what the consumer has to pay to make an acquisition. The value is what your customer gets out of the product which is, of course, the benefit. Base pricing upon the benefits that the customer perceives. Not upon your costs.

Price in the mind of the consumer has no relation to the costs to you in manufacturing the product. Your customer doesn't care how much it cost you to produce the product. This is value-based pricing. You have to calculate the delivered value the consumer gets from using the product. You want to set the price below that amount. The consumer judges value and quality from the price that they see. Take a look at your value proposition.

Price is a signal of value in comparison to alternative products in the market. You want to make sure that your distributors understand your pricing structure. When you set a price, it's much more than a dollar amount. It includes shipping and handling, perceived value. Customers need a clear picture of pricing with nothing ambiguous. If they become confused, they may go somewhere else. Customers need you to make it very clear about the total price paid. They need it to calculate a buying decision. Balancing this against the perceived value of the product.

You need to keep reminding them about the value and benefits of the product. You also want your customers to be able to describe and explain your product to others. Including its features and performance. Remember you want your customers to be brand ambassadors.

Your customers should have a mental image of the product that ties to your brand identity. They should also have a vision of themselves using the product and enjoying its benefits to them. Your marketing communications might contain this image suggesting up to the consumer. It's called behavioral awareness.

This is where we are digging into the psychology of marketing communications. Your marketing communications need to have a clear goal. Define your messages. Define the target audiences for those messages. Select the appropriate media for that message and create the promotional material. The message that you send will include the value proposition and evidence to back it up. It has to include the reasons to believe.

You might want to use a professional copywriter at this stage. The copywriter will want to know the target audience. They will benefit from your prior planning and research. You have to present that message in a way that makes the target audience feel that its written for them.

Converge on that message. The media used in the message, the value proposition, the product and everything else . So that it sells for the consumer as an individual at the time that they receive the message. With email, we can use the recipient's name. Other forms of advertising a more broad.

You have to weigh cost versus reach. Meaning how many customers you contact. Balanced with the targeting of the information sent out.

You need to match the medium to the message. Then decide on how large of a group you want to reach based upon your budget. After that decision, you can start working on the copywriting and marketing material. You can use an advertising agency to do all this, but they will still need a lot of information and guidance from you.

Social media is a great way to communicate your value proposition. Also to enhance your branding. Tie those social media programs together with your marketing strategy. Otherwise, things can go off track. Effective marketers use social media to listen to consumers and spy on them. They can also join in and interact with consumers and shape the conversation. Twitter has a search function. You can look up individual products and find out what people are saying. You can do it for your brand or company name or your personal branding. Track this 24/7 using software. Google can also do the same thing and email you every time specific terms get looked up. You can set Google to do this at specific time intervals. Once a week you might get an email with all the searches for your search term during that week. That's called Google alerts.

Once you've listened on for a while, you can find ways to join in. It has to in an authentic way. So you should only do it when you have something relevant thats going to be helpful to the consumers. Help consumers with their problems on social media. You can build a positive reputation. You want to share information that supports your value proposition. To fulfill your promotional objectives while not overdoing it.

Your company needs to have a clear social media policy defining what you can and cannot do. Social media is another channel for marketing. Consider return on investment must when comparing it to other channels. That channel can carry information and money. Either way, it's a transaction. Information sent through the channel could be about your product. Prices, availability or upcoming promotions. The beauty of social media is that it usually in real-time.

Social media can also provide a vast wealth of data on your customers. You can increase the amount of data that becomes available. Interact through the right social media channels.

Distribution channels are a means to deliver a product. Customers have particular needs about location and timing when it comes to delivery. Train your distribution partners to be most effective. They represent your brand like anybody else that you use in the business. People selling your product need merchandising skills. To explain it to your customers they may have to compare it to competing products.

The channel you use may have particular benefits. Quick delivery or customer support built-in. You can also distribute direct which makes it easier for you to keep a tight rein on your branding.

Some products suffer from a problem called feature creep. This is where the product has far too many bells and whistles. When its accumulated too many features. It ends up with the value of these features being inconsistent with the customer needs. It may be a fantastic product, but the customer finds it confusing in the end with so many features. Sometimes a new feature makes your product so much better than the competition. You do have to introduce it and in these circumstances you can go back and alter your value proposition. Make sure your customer is still getting what they want, need and expect.

Sometimes you have to present your marketing strategy in meetings. This is with clients or senior management. You should be able to present your strategy in 30 seconds or less during an elevator pitch. In this speech, you present the market conditions and the competitive situation. Who your targeting and how your positioning will convert customers. You have to be upfront and honest about your strengths and weaknesses. This is how you can gain trust.

Motivate and educate your salespeople. Your sales team need to be fans of your product, and they need to be your best brand ambassadors. They need to know your strategy and your value proposition. They need to know what the target market is and they need to know how to access that market.

Your sales team should always have a point of contact for any questions or concerns they may have. The more support you can offer them the better. You should provide them with promotional material. Websites, videos and all manner of sales literature. They need a creative brief and a branding document.

CHAPTER FOUR

SUMMARY

People make a common mistake people make when employing a designer. They have an idea in mind already that doesn't tie in with their brand identity. What's needed is a design strategy that ties in with the brand identity. Quite often in the situation, the business owner has a clear vision of what they want for their company. But they don't quite know how to get the design to that stage. They come along and say to the designer hey I've seen this neat logo or this cool website. The designer is not going to be able to tell if it fits with your brand identity or not.

Is the brand identity is the visual identity? Visual identity is only a part of the brand identity, it's a preview of the brand. You want the visual identity to show the consumers exactly what your brand is all about. Then they can make a buying decision and be happy about it after.

DESIGN AND BRAND IDENTITY

People make a common mistake people make when employing a designer. They have an idea in mind already that doesn't tie in with their brand identity. They may have seen a logo or a website somewhere that looks good. They will ask a designer to reproduce this. Without any consideration for their branding that's already in place. They hire this designer and say I've got this idea for a logo or a website and it kind of looks like this one. The designer wants to make them happy so he will go ahead and do as they asked.

What's needed is a design strategy that ties in with the brand identity. A designer cares about making things look cool or beautiful. What you need is a design that represents your brand and your core values. You need a designer that understands the principles of branding. In relation to your business. Quite often in this situation, the business owner has a clear vision of what they want for their company. But they don't quite know how to get the design to that stage. The idea for the design may come about in a brainstorming session. This enables creation of a list of definite things.

The problem is if you are making it look cool or pretty it's all subjective. Your return on investment is the bottom line, and you need it all to represent your brand. Your personal preferences in design may not be the same as your customers. You need the designers involvement in the brainstorming process. They should understand your business case and your brand identity. Its about the design outcome. For the designer, it's a discovery session. Designers need to know your value proposition. Your competition and how you make money.

They need to understand your users and customers. Designers must have a clear picture of your customer avatar. Designers need to know all the demographics. Plus other information that you have about your customers. They need to understand your culture. The atmosphere and personality of your business.

When you come along and say to the designer hey I've seen this neat logo or this cool website. The designer is going to be able to tell if it fits with your brand identity or not. If it doesn't a good designer will point that out to you and clarify that it is not suitable for your business case. You don't want a designer that's going to pander to you to make money. You need to make that clear to the designer in the first place. A brand strategy and a design strategy are the same things. The designer is trying to solve your business problem.

Is the brand identity is the visual identity? Visual identity is only a part of the brand identity, it's a preview of the brand. . The whole concept may seem pedantic. Especially when there are some famous brands with logos unrelated to the business. But those companies have massive exposure over many years. Many of them are cultural icons. Go through the correct strategic process to develop a new brand from scratch. This will speed up the acceptance of your brand by the consumer market.

It's a good idea to have a visual style guide for your brand. This will include colors, fonts, logo sizes and placements for these elements. It will also describe cases in which the logo cant appear. Also how it cant appear. This way you can have consistency across all your advertising and marketing material. It also makes it easier to communicate with designers in the future. The style guide contains information relevant to social media, website design, and stationery.

You want the visual identity to show the consumers exactly what your brand is all about. So they can make a buying decision and be happy about it after. The main components of the visual identity are the logo, color typography, and images. You want to have a master copy of that logo in storage. The colors you use are very important. Colors link with emotion. Sales data online also shows that specific colors result in more sales. So you want to keep that in mind. Take both the design and the business case into consideration.

Many decisions are subjective. Test decisions against both the customer's response and the return on investment. To do this you have to go through iterations. Test somehow on a website. Many companies don't go to that extent. They will create the brand identity and go through their design process. But won't go through an extensive testing stage.

They design a prototype brand that works for them, and then they will say okay it is what it is.

Testing out a brand is an expensive process both for time and money. Images also have to fit with the brand. A particular style of image may be most suitable, or it may be a more important subject matter. All these things combined have to represent your company's brand persona. A good designer with business knowledge can help you with this.

So let's go through it in stages. Number one is your color palette. This has to match the personality of your brand, and it's key to brand recognition.

Number two is the fonts. Depending upon the size of your business you may or may not want to use a commercial font. You can usually find a matching free font that looks very much like a commercial one. You want to keep the number of fonts low. One to three.

Number three concerns your images and photographs. You can apply a particular filter for all pictures. This gives everything a consistent look and feel. It provides everything with an element of personality.

Number four is templates. All the above can be templates. Make everything more consistent and more comfortable to do. For example, you can have a templated signature and letterhead. This way you can hand off the design work to any designer, and they will see what's required. If you've done things right designers won't be making mistakes. Like stretching or re-coloring your elements. They should never need to find any fonts to use because it's all spelled out for them.

They will have a set of rules and guidelines that make it very clear how they are to use your design elements. also your brands representation. This makes the job easier for them, and these guidelines should be very comprehensive. Even a small business should have logo guidelines. Guidelines about fonts and colors. Doing these things enables a more professional branding environment.

CHAPTER FIVE

SUMMARY

A strong brand can give your business loyal repeat customers. The process of branding has five steps. You have to define your brand drivers. These describe how the core values integrate into your marketing plan. In a competitive market with many small businesses branding won't pay off. This is because everything is too fragmented. Identify exactly who your target market is. Identify the benefits they are seeking. What they think of your product compared to the competitor's products.

Next up you have to express the brand and to do this you can create a brand persona which is a personification. To build a successful branding strategy, you have to have a solid marketing strategy in place. The two link together. Follow a step-by-step system of developing the brand and its value. Then attach those to the company, or instead attach the company to the values. Sometimes you only want to brand a feature of a product, you can brand services, and you can brand an entire company. Which approach you use depends on your marketing strategy.

At this point, you're ready to consider how to express the brand. How to create a brand name, brand identity and total customer experience. Whenever the consumers encounter the brand. When consumers encounter a new brand what strikes them first is the look and feel of the brand. The brand identity is very visual at first as that is our primary sense.

BRAND BUILDING

One of the world's biggest brands is Coca-Cola. Of the company's $170 billion plus valuation about 70 billion of it is the brand. Brands are a strategic and financial asset. They create customer loyalty and increased company value. Brands can allow you to set higher prices because of trust.

Brands have to make and keep a promise. When you keep that promise you wont need to market to loyal customers so hard. Employees are more passionate, and your company has more esteem and status. Despite this, some companies are better off not developing a brand. You may operate in a competitive market with many small businesses. Branding won't pay off because everything is too fragmented.

Branding Process

01 Define

02 Position

03 Express

04 Communicate

05 Measure

A strong brand can give your business loyal repeat customers. and the process of branding has five steps. You have to define the brand and everything about it. You have to define what the brand promises and what the core values of the company are. Simple people call it the DNA of the company. If you have other brands already, you have to define how it links to them and how it fits into your company. You have to define your brand drivers. They describe how the core values integrate into your marketing plan.

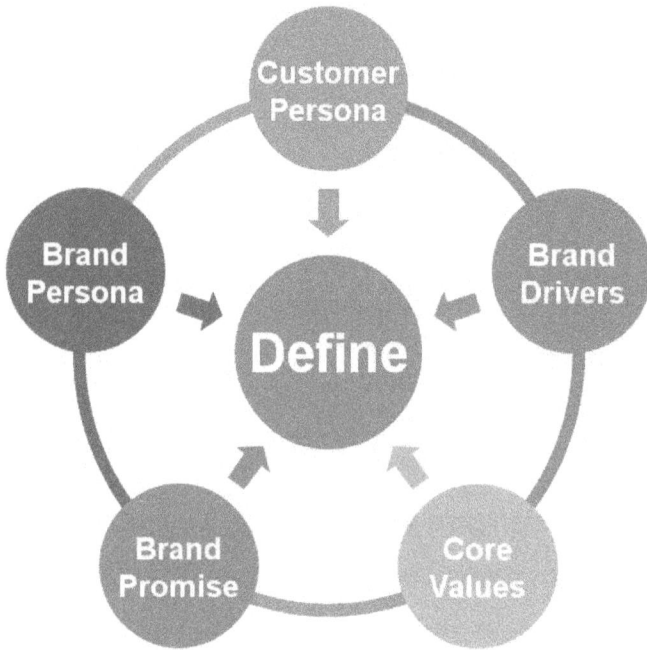

Positioning the brand shapes how the consumers think about it. You identify exactly who your target market is. Identify the benefits they are seeking. What they think of your product compared to the competitor's products.

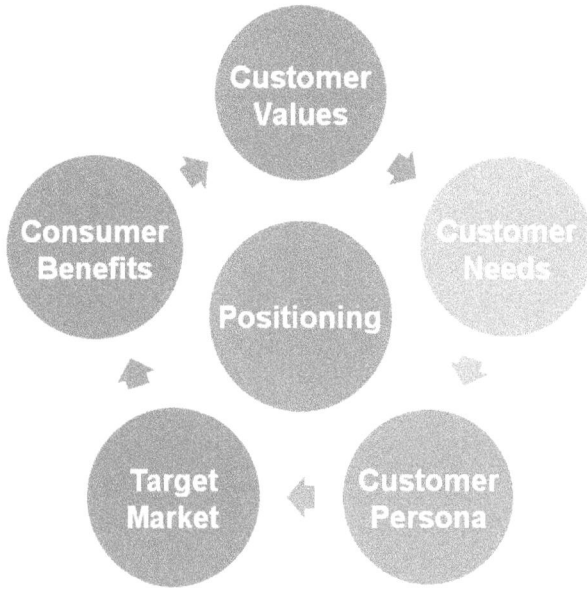

Customer Values

Consumer Benefits

Customer Needs

Positioning

Target Market

Customer Persona

Next up you have to express the brand and to do this you can create a brand persona which is a personification. You give the brand a personality and an identity. You create your logos and brand name slogans. Make it clear and easy for customers to remember the brand and its promise. You communicate the brand to build awareness of it. Continuous communication to keep a strong brand. You have to reinforce the promise in the minds of the market place consumers.

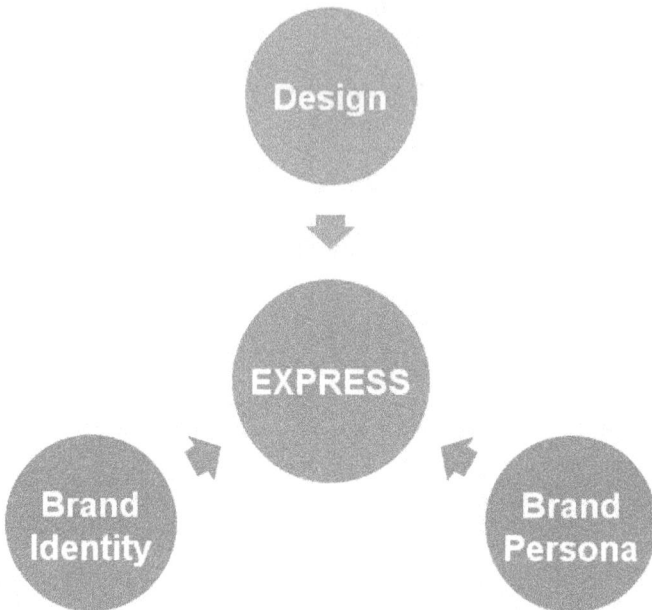

You then need to measure the value of the brand equity. As you increase and build brand equity the value of your company increases. You also want to measure the performance of the brand, is it doing what you anticipated it would do.

A healthy and robust brand can make your business more successful. To build a brand, first up we have to identify values. A brand is a promise, and that promise gets support from values. The values are the virtues of the brand that you will be communicating.

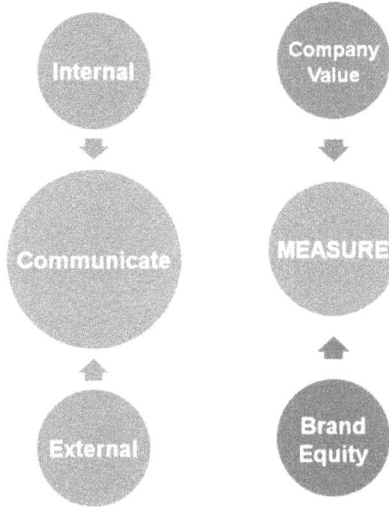

Those values are a belief system. You need to understand your marketing strategy for the business. The kinds of products and services you have on offer. Trends and opportunities in the marketplace and who your customers and competitors are.

To build a successful branding strategy, you have to have a solid marketing strategy in place. The two link together. Let's say a company is producing a new car and they decide to target the family market. So this is a family car like a station wagon. In particular, you're targeting the parents, so you want a position your car is an ideal vehicle for mums and dads. This might sound familiar if you think of Volkswagen. The people's car, except this, is the mums and dads car.

Thats your marketing strategy. You want to create a brand that delivers on the promise of being an ideal car for parents. Next you identify the fundamental values that this brand has to have for the promise to be authentic. You need to list concepts and beliefs around the parents. What does it mean to be a parent, is it hard work?

You're looking for a list of these things to shake the theme of your brand. Hard working, concern for their children, that kind of thing. You need to create a single sentence that can sum up what the brand is all about. So it could be "the parents car for families that travel together". That's not very inspirational, but you get the general idea. You want something that has a strong emotional appeal.

You have to question if the belief system of the brand links to your marketing strategy. It has to be very clear what the brand stands for and where it leads to in the future.

Building a Strong Brand

The foundation of the brand are the values. You need to define everything in the beginning stage. Brand drivers are more detailed and descriptive. They could be individual benefits or they could be beliefs about the brand. When the consumer is using the brand, these are the benefits that they perceive. You need to make an exhaustive list of phrases that suggest the brand's purpose.

We were talking about a car for a family that's ideal for mums and dads. Recalling it is the parent's car. The core value is that it celebrates parents and families being together. What else could this brand be about? So you make a list of these things that the car helps parents to do in relation to their family. The benefits that the family derives from the car. It allows parents provide for the family, takes them on family trips for fun and adventure. You can then put all these benefits into categories.

From these categories, you can start creating slogans. "Parents car helps my family enjoy the great outdoors together." That's got to be something more inspirational. These brand drivers build into the slogan. Brand drivers are emotional triggers. They help to communicate what the brand is all about. They give the brand more meaning.

You create a brand promise with its core values then you associate that with a product or a company. Branding is far more than putting a logo and a smart slogan onto your company or product. The brand and the product weave together. This is emotional and psychological.

You must be very careful not to make the mistake of slapping a logo onto the company. You need to follow a step-by-step system. Developing the brand and its value then attach those to the company. Or instead attach the company to the values. This way you are creating emotional triggers that are pleasant for the consumer.

Sometimes you only want to brand a feature of a product, you can brand services, and you can brand an entire company. You can have more than one brand within your company. If you have many brands you need to consider how they deliver value together to the consumer. When many brands exist together, it creates a brand architecture. Each brand has its relationship with the other brand. Each stands on its own as an independent entity in the consumer's mind.

Which approach you use depends on your marketing strategy. It can be less expensive to build one single brand, but it also has limitations. Youmay have a large number of brands. You will have costs involved with maintaining them. A brand architecture enables the customers to perceive the brands as you want them to. This helps you to build brand equity.

I talked about personification. This is the creation of a persona or personality for the brand. Kind of like as if the brand was a person this is who it would be. You should create a brand persona. This brand personality can talk to the character of your customer target market. In this way, your target audience can better understand the brand.

Brands with personality stand out more. We like them more because we want to have a relationship with that brand. Marketing researchers have studied the kinds of traits suitable for the brand persona. There is a research paper called dimensions of brand personality. It outlines a framework of personality traits. The five aspects are sincerity, excitement, competence, sophistication, and ruggedness. Within each of these can drilled down further. Into more specific character traits and sub traits.

You can see there's a lot of psychology involved here. We are looking at the psychology of personality traits. When determining your brand persona you need to look at the core values and brand drivers. These are the personality traits that help the consumer.

Identify Values

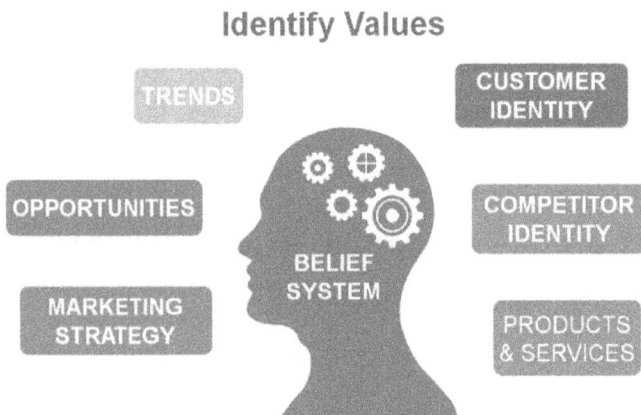

TRENDS

CUSTOMER IDENTITY

OPPORTUNITIES

COMPETITOR IDENTITY

BELIEF SYSTEM

MARKETING STRATEGY

PRODUCTS & SERVICES

The brand has to have personality traits of someone that keeps their promises. To maintain trust in its authenticity. The personality of the brand has to match that of someone who inspires trust. Remember that a brand is a promise. You have to reinforce the fulfillment of that promise. To strengthen the customer's trust.

You want loyalty from your market. Next, you must determine who they are that make up your market. Market segmentation to divides the market up. We are talking about things like gender, age, weight, height. Another way is geographic segmentation. Where they live or work or where they go for holidays. Next is behavioral segmentation which is purchasing behavior. Lifestyle or how they use a product. Finally is attitudinal segmentation. What they are thinking with regard to the benefits they are looking for.

Choose the segmentation approach most suitable. Because next- you are going to be using this to communicate to the market. During communication, you're going to win those customers over. Reinforcing the promise and its fulfillment. When people buy a product, they are purchasing a collection of its benefits. There are functional benefits, economic benefits, and emotional benefits.

When a customer purchases for a mixture of these benefits. When customers buy things, they do so because benefits fulfill the needs that they have. Form your brand promise, you can appeal to those needs if you understand your customers. It's essential to follow the steps customers take when purchasing. That helps you determine when is it appropriate to present your brand promise. During the purchasing experience.

There are some established stages during the purchasing experience. The first one is the recognition phase when the consumer recognizes they have a need to fulfill. During the next phase they search for information about products. Sometimes the one product they have in mind. Usually, they search several products and narrow it down to one. In marketing parlance this is ZMOT. During this phase, they are looking for essential features that fulfill their needs. They are seeking out information from reviews and feedback from other people.

It's at this phase that you need to communicate your brand promise. They will be narrowing the search down to one final product that they most wish to buy. After this phase when the sale has occurred, there is the post-purchase behavior phase. The consumer starts to use the product. They decide whether the brand promise delivered. They will share this information with other consumers who are still deciding what to buy. It's a feedback loop.

You need to know what role you can play in each step of the buying process. How to present your brand promise throughout. In this way, you can create a brand experience for the consumer. Positioning is crucial in marketing. The value proposition is crucial to your market positioning. The value proposition in your marketing plan relating to marketing strategy. It is like the value proposition and branding, but they are not quite the same. In branding, you have a brand promise. A statement of the benefits to the consumer offered by the brand.

Product Branding Marketing

The brands promise needs to be unique from other brands. This is brand differentiation. Differentiation and branding are crucial to brand positioning. This is what can give you an edge over your competitors, and it's both a long-term and strategic position. The value proposition in your marketing strategy is more short-term and tactical.

You have to consider the features and benefits of your products that you are emphasizing. Also the marketing strategy. Consider the brand drivers that resonate best with your consumer market avatar. You now should have your brand determined including values, drivers and persona. You have your brand positioned in the market and linked to your marketing strategy. At this point, you're ready to consider how to express the brand. How to create a brand name, brand identity and total customer experience. Whenever the consumers encounter the brand.

When you choose a name for your brand it has to reflect the values and purpose of the brand. It has to create a connection with the brand persona. It has to be unique and maintain the differentiation. It should also be simple and easy to say and memorable. If necessary, it should also fit in with other brands in your brand architecture.

Despite all this many of the world's most famous brand names have no connection with what they do or what they sell. Many of the brand names are nonsense. Even many very successful brands have logos that have no connection at all with a product or company. Think of Shell oil for example. I suppose a shell may connect with fossil fuel, but for most people there is no connection there.

Think of Sony or Apple. Those company names have no connection with the products that they sell. Those brands are still very successful. Its all a rule of thumb and heuristic. None of this is set in stone and none of it is a guarantee of success, as with anything in business.

When consumers encounter a new brand what strikes them first is the look and feel of the brand. the brand identity is very visual as that is our primary sense. That's why logos are so important and a logo can take many forms. It can be abstract, can contain words and it can be quite artistic. When designing a logo it's best to hire a professional designer. Let them know all about your brand values. Brand promise, brand persona and the persona of your consumer. A good designer will need this information to make a relevant design.

The designer will create different versions of the logo. Black-and-white and color. In different sizes for social media, stationery and use on websites. The designer will also help you choose the fonts for use with the brand, how to use text formatting and layout. And also image guidelines including what filters to use with images. Black-and-white or color, illustrations or photographs. What particular style for the illustrations. Standardize it to strengthen the brand.

Slogans and speaking. The conversation should also have a standard voice to match the brand persona. This brand persona, when it speaks is talking to the customer persona. It needs to be appealing to the psyche of the customer. You will create a beautiful brand and everything will fit together. It doesn't matter if it's not focused upon the customer avatar, you must remember that.

Consumers that buy your products go through the brand experience. In each step of their experience is a touch point. It allows you to reinforce the brand promise. This creates a closer relationship with the consumer. Look at your customer avatar. Consider what the touch points are are during a standard brand experience. Once you know what the specific touch points are you can go back to your list of brand drivers. Decide which brand driver to apply to each touch point.

Each phase of that purchasing experience has its benefits that you can derive for the brand. As a marketer, you should know that you have a role to play in each step of the consumer experience. Know how to weave your brand into that experience. Your brand maintains its authenticity by fulfilling that brand promise. Your staff and employees have to understand the brand promise. Then they know how to present it to customers. You have to train them and reinforce the brand promise in the minds. Your staff have to believe in your brand, as your customers do.

You will need to develop training programs about the brand. Have different programs for different types of employees. The employees need to know what the brand promise is. How it links to company's values and the drives the customer's experience. Your staff needs to know about the brand identity and brand persona. They should also know the customer persona. They need to understand how they should look, think, feel and act.

Your brand identity needs to be visible throughout the company. Staff must have it in mind. Many companies also have a brand champion. Brand ambassadors who serve to inspire and train the other staff. The other staff can model their behavior of these people.

So many companies are intimate with their brand and what it stands for. Staff from the beginning can have characteristics aligned with the brand. You should be looking for opportunities to reinforce the brand in the mind of your staff every day. They should have full confidence that the brand fulfills its promise. A brand book is like a manual. That is a guide to the brand and its elements. It is a strict guide to the brand identity including everything about how to use the logo. The look of the website, how social media works, everything that the designer has created. It should also iterate the core promise of the brand. The values, persona, writing style, and conversational style.

This brand book is crucial as a reference for your employees. Also other companies that you do business with. To present your brand thus making it a strong brand. You don't want this information to be `vague you want it to be very detailed and definite. This brand manual will be more effective if it is inspirational. If it contains stories about the brand. Also examples of the success of the brand promise for consumers. If there are examples of staff implementing the brand, that's a good idea to include.

The brand promise is everything. What are the benefits to the consumer that your current products deliver? Are they the same as those provided by your brand promise? You want to remove any gaps in your marketing. You need to make sure that your products are not under or over-featured. Make a list of all the benefits of your products and all the features of those products. Then, for each feature, list the advantage that it has to the consumers. Recall that the benefits are functional, economic, emotional or self-expressive. Try to connect those benefits with the brand drivers.

This is to strengthen the alignment of brand. If the products are not aligned, you will need to develop new ones. You can use the process to create products that align with the brand promise. The consumer interprets an effective brand as representing how the product will perform. And it all needs to be consistent with the brand. Some of your marketing campaigns will be communicating the core brand promise.

Others will communicate your brand positioning. Others will focus on features and benefits of the products.

Your brand message has to be relevant to your target audience. Group your customers according to demographic, geographic, behavioral and attitudinal characteristics. You need to be aware of which segment you're communicating with. To project the correct emotional benefits. The brand drivers determine what you're communicating for. What specific message you want to include.

You also need to determine where you are communicating. Your choice of media is not random. Determine media by the message and its appropriateness. These decisions come down to the ROI and how effective the medium and message are in that respect.

When designing your message you have to refer to the brand book to make sure everything aligns. This may sound complicated. If so present it in a flowchart. Using a flowchart can keep everything more organized and clear throughout each stage. Then you always know what you need to do next and what you should have done already. You can also see how elements are interdependent. Also which ones are not necessary for your particular task.

Your sites if they adhere to the brand book will have a similar look and feel about them. This is what you want, and you don't want customers to become confused. You want them focused to make your brand strong. If you're using social media sites then follow your rules about communication style. This is so the brand personality is clear. You should be aware of the role of each channel.

Each of these media channels, be it a blog or a social media site, is a touch point for the customer experience. This again should link to a different brand driver. You can also experiment with the various social media channels. Using different drivers . Find which provides the best ROI for each one. In this way, you can optimize your branding and marketing through the channels.

Even the packaging of the product is crucial to branding. It can result in more sales and improve the perception of your brand. Promotional material can go inside the packaging. You can think of ways to encourage the consumers to communicate your brand. Including to other consumers that may not have purchased yet. You can communicate the benefits of your brand. What makes it better than competitors brands?

Digital products don't have packaging. They do have download pages, and they do have a marketing funnel after the sale has taken place. This is in a way the digital version of packaging. The packaging allows you to influence your customers and alter the brand perception. Do it right, and you can increase brand loyalty.

Measure your brand performance. You need to know the general awareness of your brand. Using market research you want to know how many people recognize your logo or slogan. How strong is your brand within the target audience? Does the target audience understand your brand? Do they know what differentiates your brand from competitors?

You need to figure out if the consumers understand your brand the way you want them to. If they are communicating to other consumers the way you want. If they aren't, you may have to figure out why. Have you been keeping up and maintaining the brand promise? If you haven't people will feel let down by the brand. They won't believe the brand promise and will no longer see the brand is authentic. They will also communicate this to other consumers.

You can measure this in the marketplace. You also need to measure the brand inside the company. With your employees so they can do an excellent job of communicating the brand for you. Another thing is determining if competitors are abusing the brand. Discover if anyone has used any of your logos or other creatives, which can weaken your brand. Has anyone presented your brand in a bad light in memes on social media for example?

Is there any way you can weaken a competitors brand? In a sly way without breaking the law? by all means, you should if it strengthens your brand and puts it in a good light. Bbe sure there won't be a response from the competitor that you can't answer to. Sometimes brands are complementary, and you can cooperate with competitors. This often happens in sponsorship and sports. There you see many brands working together in promotions.

The world changes and brands must change also. Your brand is not monolithic and permanent, while it must be strong, change at some point will come. It's not unusual for companies to upgrade their logos, for example. Usually, it will be the same design but with some modification or simplification. This is to keep the brand consistent with changes in the marketplace and the consumer psyche. These changes should not be too often, or the brand will dilute.

You can hire brand stewards to track the brand and its effectiveness. The brand stewards job is to make sure the brand is consistent and strong throughout. Also that staff do not start implementing the brand identity in a wrong way. In a small company the CEO may take on this role himself, but in larger organizations, it is a job for an individual. You can have brand champions. who are internal ambassadors for the brand and serve as models for the other staff. There can be an annual brand audit to determine if the brand is performing. If it isn't what change must occur?

Chapter Six

Summary

The core values of your brand tell the consumers what your brand stands for. They will attract consumers with the same values. You select those brand values by choosing words that match with your core beliefs. The brand vision is your vision of where you see the company being in the future. Finding your brand vision and statement can be time-consuming. It's well worth the effort. People become fans, fanatical supporters.

What are your customer's expectations? If there is no differentiation their focus will be the price, you want to get it off the price and onto the value. You need to fulfill the expectations but go beyond, fulfill their desires. Step one is to define what your company is all about. Define your core values and beliefs. For example, a health food company that is against factory farmed chickens. This is going to stick in the minds of customers more than one that says they promote organic food.

Next up is the customer and you need to identify their emotional need. Identify the customer's most profound emotional need. this needs to align with the core values of your brand.

THE BRAND PROMISE

The core values of your brand tell the consumers what your brand stands for. They will attract consumers with the same values. You need those consumers to become familiar with your core values. Rather than only trying to present them on your website. If must find consumers that share those values. They will become enthusiastic fans and ambassadors of your brand.

Amazon, for example, has core values of simplicity, trust, courage, and ownership. For Amazon, trust plays a significant factor. Amazon tried to build these values into its website funnel and sales process. There is consistency across Amazon.

You select those brand values by choosing words that match with your core beliefs. You want to establish these values when first developing your brand. They are foundational throughout the brand development process. Even an established brand can come up with more brand values.

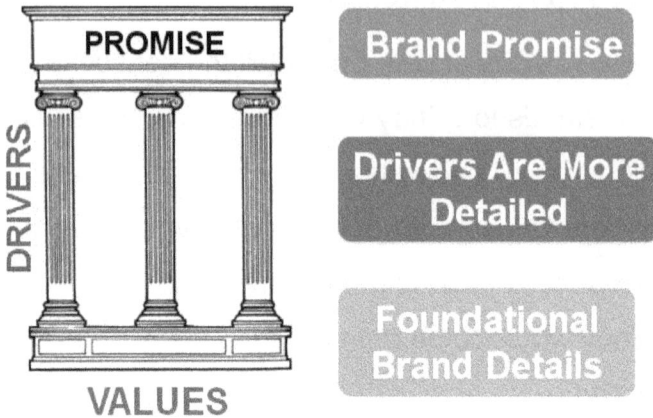

The brand vision is your vision of where you see the company being in the future. You will develop a vision statement. Microsoft, for example, has the statement "a computer on every desktop in every home". So you want to figure something out for your company. Notice how it's a short sentence. Instagram, for example, has the vision statement "capture and share the world's moments". It's very brief, memorable and it sets a firm clear goal.

Once you have a brand vision that becomes a goal and a focus that you can strive toward. That vision may change in time as you meet goals, but it should not chang because it's too difficult to get to. Remember for many years Amazon was not turning a profit.

Finding your brand vision and statement can be time-consuming. It's still well worth the effort. The brand promise is something different. It's your promise to the consumer. It aligns with the consumer persona. You want those customers to become passionate fans of your brand. People become fans of all kinds of brands and companies. Apple is the most obvious one. People actually become fans, fanatical supporters of a telephone manufacturer. That's quite odd when you think of it that way. Technology is a great selling point.

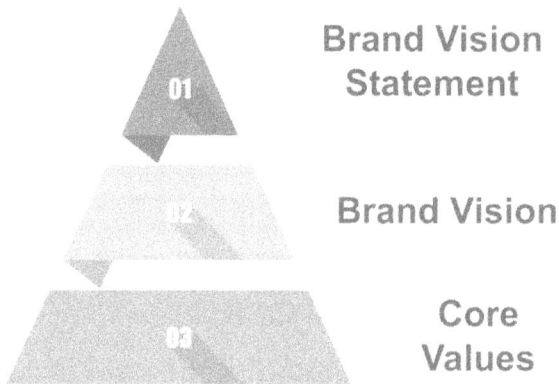

Brand Vision Statement

Brand Vision

Core Values

You need to get the brand promise right, and it needs to emphasize your differentiation. Otherwise, you're another company selling the same product or services in the same way. Distinguishing yourself from the crowd is essential. How do you stand out, what's different about you, what's better about you? What have you got that the competition has not?

If you can't distinguish yourself you become another commodity in the market. The act of branding introduces differentiation. The more quality you can introduce to the consumer. The more needs you can tap into through that differentiation. T

he more successful and strong your brand will become. Proper differentiation can overcome price objections. It can get you long-lasting customer loyalty.

While it's always good to bring in new customers you need to nurture the ones that you already have. You need to build a relationship. Cultivate the connections with those existing customers. They will help you to get more new customers. A lot of it is mutual communication and content. You will find if you do it right many of the challenges of competition fade away.

One example is when companies make themselves stand out with customer service. They bend over backward to make sure that consumer is happy. They are easy to communicate with and fast with feedback. This differentiates them from their competitors and strengthens the brand. Companies like this develop evangelical customers. Leverage your customer service like this. Then the number of competitive companies in your industry will decrease. You will still need to find and other means to differentiate. Some competitors in other companies will have high levels of customer service.

You can't build those evangelists by telling them things about your product or brand. It has to come through experience, trust, and interaction with your brand. You do have to deliver. So they will become your unpaid sales team.

Think of an army of people wearing your T-shirts with your brand on the front. With stickers with your logo stuck on the fridge.

Apple provides excellent customer service. They also pack features into their consumer products. Those features differentiate them from other companies with excellent customer service. Many Apple customers will wear an Apple T-shirt with pride. It becomes a trend. You need to consider the individual identities of the consumers . You need to consider their aspirations and how you can help to fulfill those. Apple again as an example has great appeal to the digital design community.

You also need to create a buzz and start up a conversation when you deliver your product. You want to over deliver and create an experience. The consumers will remember for a long time with positive connotations. Think about this about your product and how you're promoting it. Rather than doing the same promotion as everybody else. What angle can you take that your competitors are not?

TRUST

01 EMOTIONAL TRIGGERS

02 BELIEFS

03 BENEFITS

BRAND
DRIVERS

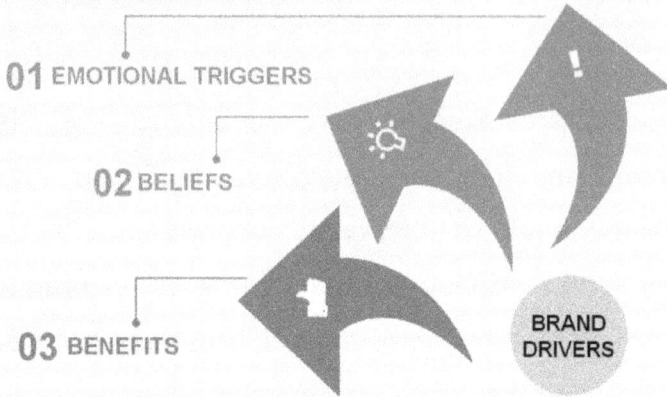

What are your customer's expectations? You need to know that so then you can exceed those expectations. You have to do this in a way that introduces distinction. If there is no differentiation their focus will be the price, you want to get it off the price and onto the value.

You need to set your standard above that of customer satisfaction. You need to fulfill the expectations but go beyond, fulfill their desires. They always desire more than they expect, can you deliver it? If you can do that, then your product becomes a premium in the consumer's mind.

With their desires fulfilled you will have repeat customers. At this point you can develop a relationship with these customers. Then you can start to meet their unexpected needs. You can start doing things for them that they were not anticipating. But there has to be an element of intimacy for you to know which things to do. Working at this level. It becomes a relationship that appeals to the customer's identity. Working at the identity level or create fans and brand ambassadors.

Word-of-mouth on the Internet has become much more prevalent than in the past. On the Internet word-of-mouth is viral. You can tap into that by exceeding your customer's expectations. By exceeding their desires. Working at the level of their unexpected needs. Doing it in such a way that makes them perceive you as being extraordinary. This will make them your brand ambassadors and fans. It's double-edged as if you do things wrong then you are going to be viral for all the wrong reasons.

You have it clear by now that you need to know how to position your brand. You need to be the brand that your prospective customers think of first. That they feel a sense of trust towards it is most important. You need to stand out as head and shoulders above the competition. Especially when your customer is in the research phase. This is how your brand should position your brand.

Step one is to define what your company is all about. Define your core values and beliefs. They are principles that you believe in as a company. What are the things you are against? This can be more powerful in the mind of your customer. For example, a health food company that is against factory farmed chickens. It is going to stick in the minds of customers more than one that says they promote organic food. So you need to address that for your particular business. Whether you are selling books or shoes or a car wash service.

Identify what it is that your brand does that can differentiate you. Be different from the competition within the marketplace. You also want to identify the defining characteristics of your company. What are its strong points? A swot analysis is what's required. Do this before positioning your brand

DEMOGRAPHICS

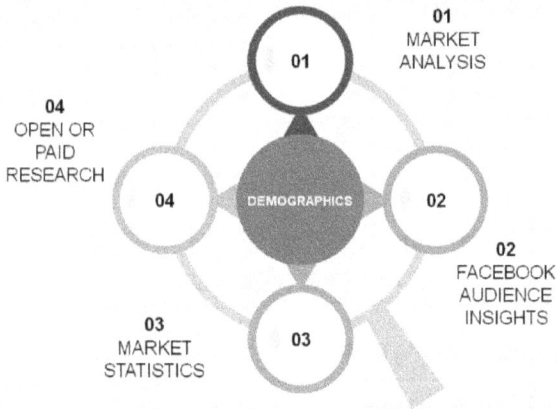

01
MARKET
ANALYSIS

01

04
OPEN OR
PAID
RESEARCH

04

DEMOGRAPHICS

02

02
FACEBOOK
AUDIENCE
INSIGHTS

03
MARKET
STATISTICS

03

Next up is the customer and you need to identify their emotional need. What is it they want under the surface? Someone selling chocolates isn't going to sell the delicious aroma of the chocolate. Instead, they're going to sell the delight of your wife. As she enjoys the delightful aroma of the gift you've bought for her. It has to cut right down to the emotional bone of the issue. Identify the customers deepest emotional motive for purchasing.

Identified the customer's most profound emotional need. Then align it with the core values of your brand. So long as you've chosen the right customer for your brand, this alignment should be easy to recognize. If it isn't then you have targeted the wrong market demographic. Create a bond between your core values and the most profound emotional need of your customer. That's where the magic is.

Determine if you're fulfilling the brand promise. Identify the expectations of the customers toward your brand. Are you exceeding the deepest desires of the customers? If you are fulfilling the brand promise, then your customers should be happy. If they are not happy you need to identify why.

So there we have it. that's how to develop your brand promise, it's complicated but a logical process.

CHAPTER SEVEN

SUMMARY

Now it's time to discuss brand differentiation. I'm going to give you three ways to make your product different from your competitors. The first way is very obvious and that's price. One means of differentiation is design. Adding new features and benefits to the design of a product or service. The third means of differentiation is marketing and branding. If you're using a shotgun approach and broad marketing you're not going to be able to segment people. You're not going to be able to zoom in at the crucial point of sale. Apart from telling a story, you have to focus on your USP. Your unique selling proposition has to be exactly that - unique.

BRAND DIFFERENTIATION

The world's biggest brands differentiate their products as much as possible. From the competition. They don't slap a logo on any of commodity product and put it up there against other companies. This is what many small-time retailers and online sellers tend to do. Because they are not familiar with the branding process. The big firms are companies like Apple, IBM, Mobil. They spend so much time and money on product differentiation. Also brand differentiation, because they know all that time and effort pays off.

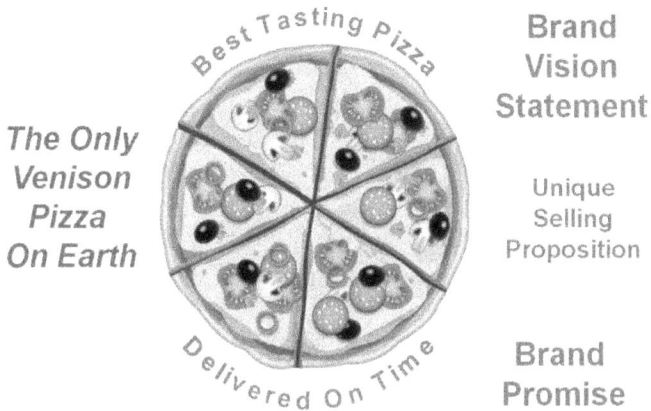

I'm going to give you three different examples or ways that you can do the same thing to build a strong brand. There are more than three ways to do it, but here we to focus on the big three. I can't even say these are the three best ways, but here we go. The first way is very obvious and that's price.

Sell your products on as many different market bases and avenues as possible. From on your own domain to e-commerce sites like Amazon and eBay. If you have affiliates, then they'll be on websites all over the world. Price is not the best way to differentiate your product, but it is a self-explanatory one. If you are a small time drop shipper selling on Amazon price is not the best way to differentiate your products.

Many of the big car companies sell very similar products. They don't try and beat each other on price because it endsup making no profit . No return on investment. They are always looking at different ways to differentiate the brand. Not the price only. Manufacturers, have a lot to gain by differentiating on price. That's because of mass production. Price is your significant advantage. Someone who is selling branded products does not have this advantage.

The second means of differentiation is design. Adding new features and benefits to the design of a product or service. This is an excellent means of differentiation. From changing a color or a shape, to improving the actual function or performance of a product. You want to introduce things that make your product stand out and worth paying attention to. The big brands do this. Before slapping their logo on a product they add new features and more value for the target market. New and unique features.

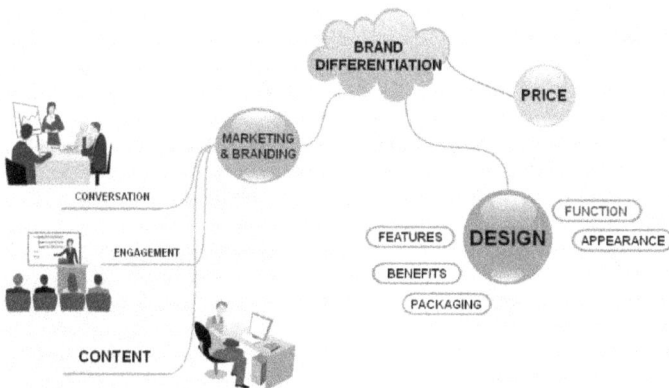

The third means of differentiation is marketing and branding. Many business people overlook branding and marketing. bThese are two of the most essential things in business. This is where most big brands spend most of their budget. They have an avatar or persona of the ideal customer that buys their products and services. They target that persona with content, engagement, and conversation. The customer then links the value of this product to them. If you're someone looking to sell branded products this is what you have to become an expert at.

You have to know the exact persona. The exact personality that you are selling to and that your product serves. This will help you stand out from the competition, get it right. If you're using broad marketing you're not going to be able to segment or target people. You're not going to be able to zoom in at the crucial point of sale. It's important who you know that target is. Then you can target your advertising and the demographics of placement.

You can show pictures of that customer persona using your product. Deriving value from its benefits. Then the customers are going to see that and then they are going to think hey that's me I want that stuff. You know the personality. Then you also know what social media influences are most suited to your marketing mix.

Ask yourself exactly who is it that on targeting is going to buy my product? Where it will they buy my product, will it be on Amazon from entering keywords? If they do that and my product shows up what will make them want to buy mine rather than others? This is the kind of mindset you have to have when launching new products. You have to determine how to make yourself stand out from your competitors. How is your product different from product X?

Let's move away from product branding. Let's consider somebody trying to get get a job as a software developer. They might set up a blog as a portfolio. They may list a whole lot of software languages, and development skills that they can offer. They may offer Java, Microsoft, JavaScript and python skills. Thinking that then they can apply for a whole lot of different jobs and a bunch of different companies. They may then list a whole lot of various applications. Such as e-commerce and artificial intelligence. Database design, and management, mobile at design and android design. So this person might have a beautiful website and portfolio, but they spread too wide.

It also shows that they don't know who their target business is. They are not targeting any particular customer. They may think this gives them more opportunity for getting job interviews. It doesn't because its an untargeted approach.

It would make more sense for this person to first assess what type of company they want to work for. What kind of industry they want to work for. For example, they may decide to work in e-commerce. They may select finance or artificial intelligence. Once they have chosen one single industry, then they can look at their strengths as a programmer. Choose one primary language say python for example. So, on their blog, they are a python expert, with expertise in e-commerce. It's much more targeted, and now they can go after that single type of company.

It's the same marketing products. This is a way to decrease competition as well. The guy taking the shotgun approach is competing with everybody. It's a nightmare. The guy that's targeted only has a small fraction as many competitors. He can present himself as an expert. A targeted product can present as one of the best for that market.

Going back to our software developer example, which is a service business. Because it's a service business is has lots of competition. Anybody can contact start-ups or retailers and offer themselves as a developer. A service business is a real easy one to start, but they have a lot of competition.

One of the first things you need to do is come up with a list of the most common competitors. You want your sales team to know the difference between you and all those firms. Know everything you can about these companies. Narrow down to your local city and find local web developers. E-commerce specialists, app developers. The ones that come up on the first page of Google are the biggest competitors. You then want to look at the tools that allow people to do that specific job. So for web developers, its wix, lead pages and that kind of thing.

You need to look at why you and your team are better than that tool. Look at competitive products, talk to the sales team and get demo versions. The next thing is to improve the service or product. You can experiment, and brainstorm, and you can also talk to and survey the customers. You can look at your competitor's support forums, they are a great place to look. Find what you're potential customers dislike or find challenging about your competition. You can offer them exactly what they want.

Many of these markets have become flooded. Web development for small to medium businesses. It is overrun with a surplus of developers. Software as a service, app development. Digital agencies for small businesses are all flooded markets.

You need to find a new market that doesn't know about you. So once again it may be that these companies that do web development are doing it across the board for anybody. What if you target a specific niche industry. Then offer web development and digital services for that industry alone. When you're up against these guys and you're specialized you can beat them. Every time because your brand differentiated.

If you can't improve the product and can't take the entire market then improve your product and target a niche. You also don't want to use clichés in your promotions. You don't want to be as good as everyone else, that's the wrong mentality. If you're only as good as everyone else, then you're nobody. You want to target a specific audience and specialize. Then you know and speak the language of that audience.

Look at the sales funnels and sales procedures of your competitors. Are they all doing the same thing? If they are, if there is a general trend, that allows you to differentiate and do it better. Instead of inviting a client into your office to run through a questionnaire why not ask them out for lunch. What we are talking about here is innovation.

One thing you want to do is tell your customers a story. A story can make you unique and can explain why your product and company are different. Some stories prove to be more successful in sales and marketing, and I'm not going to go into that here. People form an emotional connection and its part of the "persona" communication.

Apart from telling a story, you have to focus on your USP. Your unique selling proposition has to be - unique. There is more to brand differentiation than the USP. But you still have to have one, and you need to weave it into your story. You also need to identify the core need of your customer persona. Ask yourself are you fulfilling that need? How is what you do fulfilling the customer's needs?

If your brand identity meets the core need of the market then your brands differentiated. Your customer is researching and investigating the options. They only want to choose one product that is the best. That's in the ideal circumstance, and you want to be that best product, the only way is by differentiation. Differentiation is one of the most vital tools. When branding and marketing your company, product or service. It's not optional.

CHAPTER EIGHT

SUMMARY

There is a saying in marketing; your brand is what people say about you when you're not in the room. There is a big difference between branding and marketing.

Branding is strategic whereas marketing is more tactical. Visibility can take many forms. It's done with digital advertising or with T-shirts, posters and fridge stickers.

Establish your brand identity. You have your brand design manual, you're supposed to stick with that. Make your brand clean and robust. A marketer testing design elements is going to find all sorts of things that work and things that don't. This process will give you an advantage over the majority of companies. They go through the brand development process and accept it as the final product. Consumers interact with your company through the advertising channels and promotional material. They should be aware that they are dealing with your brand.

You can also test different unique selling propositions. Test your core values and differentiation against real customer responses online. Once you know your core value, you can hold people accountable to it. Staff and employees can make intelligent decisions when they know your core values. It's not always easy to engage the target clients for a new business. Figure out the products you want to provide. They give these targeted customers the best value.

COMMUNICATING THE BRAND

There is a saying in marketing; your brand is what people say about you when you're not in the room. It doesn't matter if you're somebody working for a firm or engaging with clients you are the actual brand. It doesn't matter if it's a subcontractor, someone at the point of sale, or somebody working on the front desk. They all represent the brand. If somebody is working for you that person as part of your brand whatever their job is. Your brand persona reflects in your company culture.

There is a big difference between branding and marketing. Your brand needs to be unique, and the marketing is how you communicate that. Brand communication is important inside and outside the company. Your team, your staff need, to be brand ambassadors that bring others on board with the brand. Expectations need to be set so that everybody knows they are accountable.

Branding is strategic whereas marketing is tactical. Branding is broad. Marketing is stuff like emails and advertising graphics, various processes. Marketing should be projecting the brand in the right voice. Consumers have to know exactly what to expect. The brand has to be authentic.

Look at McDonald's versus Burger King. McDonald's offers more of an experience to the customers. They have Ronald the clown and play areas, and it's all much more exciting for kids. Burger King is a restaurant that sells burgers. They have beautiful pictures on the wall, and it's all branded in the same way. But the experience is less than at McDonald's.

It could be then that McDonald's has a stronger brand than Burger King. Because it's more differentiated in the customer's mind. It's only a few minor marketing differences. If you want an authentic brand, you can't present it as something that it's not. You have to find your unique brand promise that gives value to your consumers. Then you have to deliver that value and fulfill the brand promise.

If you say you've got the best customer service then when I phone your company I don't want to wait. I don't want voicemail or some automated robot talking to me. You say you have the best burgers. You've got a big picture on the wall of a giant delicious burger. When I buy one I don't want some tiny little thing that tastes like the cardboard packaging. If your brand has unique products and services. If it makes big promises and fulfills those big promises, then what you have is a stronger brand.

Visibility is also important. You have to stay in front of those customers and stand out as genuine and unique. You have to make sure that you are who you say you are. Always visible. Visibility can take many forms. Its done with digital advertising. It can done with T-shirts, posters and fridge stickers. The customer has to remember your brand value. Once you fulfil your brand promise you need to keep reminding them that that's what you do.

When you're excellent, you become unforgettable. You need to set that expectation within your company about the brand. Then you need to tell the customers that that's what you are. You need to set your company apart and communicate that. Consider what pain points might exist for your consumers. Look at competitors support forums and blogs to find pain points. You have them as well, and you need to identify them and rectify those inefficiencies.

Find out what pain points the actual consumers have. Consider what solutions you can offer. Communicate to those consumers how you can fix the pain points. Pain points are bottlenecks, and when doing a brand audit, you need to find them. Find what the solution is for that problem for your customers.

There are many design factors in online branding. Color being one aspect first comes to mind. Color has emotional connotations. There are general trends in consumer behavior related to color use. Marketers online test colors. Including the responsiveness of the consumer on things like buy now buttons. Much of this testing is already done for you, and there is no reason to reinvent the wheel.

With things like colors and design it's very easy to fall into the trap of being an aesthetic or trendy. The scientific marketer will test all these things and use what gets the best ROI. The problem here is that we are trying to maintain a strong brand. What gets the most ROI may not gel with our brand. So in these cases, you're going to have to decide. Do you use a feature that dilutes your brand or brand message, or do you go with the immediate ROI benefits?

You have established brand identity. You have your brand design manual, you're supposed to stick with that. Make your brand clean and robust. A marketer testing design elements is going to find all sorts of things that work and things that don't. Things will work under some circumstances and not under others. You can perform the testing before brand identity and branding design. That's the ideal circumstance. By testing, you will find that things change and your brand will never have perfect ROI and design.

You want to put your logo everywhere and use your design fonts everywhere that you can. Design your initial branding using the principles of brand development. Then once you have the full package get into the digital testing and tracking. Then change the whole thing for ROI. You want to optimize your brand design for return on investment. That means testing different logos. Once you've found the best performer then tweak it. Testing different styles and features. It's the same with fonts, you can do AB split testing, and you can do multivariate testing. In this way, the initial design of your brand can sharpen and develop. You may end up with something very like the original brand. You may end up with something different.

This process will give you an advantage over the majority of companies. They go through the brand development process and accept it as the final product. But think about it when the Air Force buys a jet, a new fighter jet design they don't start using the thing. It goes through a complicated, expensive and time-consuming testing and breaking in period. You need to do the same thing with your brand using AB split testing and multivariate testing. You will end up with a brand that's optimized for return on investment. Where your competitors will end up with the brand that looks pretty but may not perform so well.

Okay so don't be slack on the testing. iIt's essential that that's done. You may want to find a designer with some expertise in that area and hand it over to them. This brand design is going to be all over your company. On email signatures, business cards, letterheads, websites and packaging. It's going to be on your social media and your pay per click advertising campaigns. So you want to get it right and not settle for something dished up by some designer. The brand development process on its own is not enough, and you have to test and improve.

Whenever the consumers interact with your company. Through the advertising channels and promotional material. They should be aware tthey are dealing with your brand. It should be obvious in their minds that it's your brand they are interacting with. So these brand elements have to be well placed. Your email signature is a prime real estate. There is no reason why they can't include video, photographs, and links to social media. You can test all that stuff.

They say you can't be all things to everyone. You can target segments of the market online. With different design elements and different branding elements. In some respects, testing eliminates the need for a lot of market research. But you should still do that research, of course. Understand your market. I mean when designing the brand elements. When it comes to testing that, market research gives your baseline from which to begin.

Use focus groups to understand the perception of your consumers during communication. This helps in developing your buyer persona. Build as fuller picture of your buyer persona as possible. All their habits, likes and dislikes. Where they like to hang out, the type of friends they have. When you communicate to the market zoom in and communicate to that persona. You have this avatar, and you can test the design elements directed at the persona. It gives you a starting point.

Your competitors whether they like it or not have already done a lot of testing for you. If they haven't done it on purpose, the market has performed it upon them. You may leapfrog in some circumstances by seeing competitors successes and failures. This is very common and online marketing. When somebody introduces a new design innovation. It can often spread across the whole internet in a matter of weeks.

You can also test different unique selling propositions. This is on a wider scale than checking design elements. In copywriting, to test different USP's is not an unusual idea. Copywriters will test headlines, stories, power words and keywords, all manner of things. They also test design elements like the colors, fonts, and images. You can do all this very fast using paid traffic and statistical testing software. This makes the brand development process much more accurate. You can actually test your core values and differentiation. In real time against real customer responses online.

A company that isn't doing this may be following a proven and well-honed path. But they are not optimizing their brand. Core values are critical and not some marketing trend. The core values are a fundamental belief of your brand persona. It may be something summed up in a single word like excellence. For other companies, it might be health and vitality or integrity. Take a look at your product line. Think about what your fundamental core values should be for your brand.

Once you know that core value, you can hold people accountable to it. Once your staff and employees know your core values they can make informed decisions. They can interpret the brand way you want them to. Core values present a focal point for engagement. You also want to communicate a story. Once you've found the best story for your brand, you can tell it over and over again. Story telling is a science. Worthy of further investigation and its own book.

Many people that do personal branding have a story that they tell it over and over. I'm thinking of Arnold Schwarzenegger. The stories he tells about how we went to California. With his dream of becoming a world-famous athlete and how he had to work in construction. He explains that story over and over all the time. It's something he's figured out as part of his personal branding. I'm sure there are plenty of things that he doesn't tell people about.

It's the same with your product or company. You want to have a story that's interesting, enticing and encouraging. Find the story that works best and tell it over and over again. This is your brand story. It makes your brand more engaging, and it makes your brand persona more personal and intimate. Your brand story, your brand core values and your brand slogan all need to tie together. Now imagine a brand for example that only has core values, or that only has a slogan. As you're developing the brand, it will be at that stage. Then compare that to a brand that has everything going for it with all these things developed. It's a huge difference. Develop a brand story. Some people can do this job for you if you don't have the inclination.

The elements of the brand have to fit together and at the same time be simple enough to communicate fast and easy. If you're running ad campaigns on social media or search you want your logo and brand elements to be simple. At the same time, they have to convey who you are. You can do brainstorming sessions to develop features and improvements for your brand. You can use the Internet to test them.

Your advertising campaign should be direct and straightforward. Conveying only the information thats needed. When you do these campaigns you must always capture the data. You don't want to make things too tricky with lots of forms to fill out. People won't bother. The same goes for your logo. It needs to be minimal and straightforward. This also makes it easier to remember.

You can brainstorm all this stuff beforehand in staff meetings. But it comes down to testing as I have already said. You have to communicate your expectations. Your team members are going to be your brand ambassadors, and you will need to reward them for getting it right. You can sit down and discuss with them what they would like as a reward. Don't make any assumptions about what motivates your team or your customers. Your entire organization needs engagement starting at the top.

Make your brand ambassadors proud of the job that they do. Make sure they have whatever promotional material that they need. You need to communicate your expectations to them. Set up internal engagement programs. Where they can talk to each other and brainstorm improvements. Then reward and install those improvements. You need to know what motivates these brand ambassadors.

There needs to be open communication and engagement where you can ask questions and have them ask of you. You don't want to be a know it all or arrogant. You want engaged employees committed to brand success.

It's not always easy to engage the target clients for a new business. You want to make sure that you're dealing with the most targeted. You can do a quick consultation to find out who they are and if they are a fit for your product. Figure out the products you want to provide. They give these targeted customers the best value. You can do a full brand audit and figure out a particular market segment is worth going after. You want longevity and customers that are going to be with you and your brand for the long haul.

CHAPTER NINE

SUMMARY

A lot of brick and mortar retail businesses are closing down. But look at the thousands of people with e-commerce stores online or who are doing business on Amazon FBA. There are more people doing retail now than there were when all the brick and mortar shops were still open. Consumer brands are meeting the demand of online shoppers. By meeting their needs, you can capitalize on the growth in the market.

It's a cycle of testing, learning and failing in marketing. Technology allows you to speed that cycle up. If we can look at the total market and get the full picture, that's going to lead to better forecasting models.

Somehow we have to connect all the marketing data to get an accurate picture. A connected system that talks between segments. Marketing executives are becoming more cross-functional in their organizations. They have to deal with business strategy, commercial impact, and brand vision.

BRANDING RESULTS

For retail consumer products. There's a lot of focus on e-commerce technology in the industry at present. A lot of brick and mortar retail businesses closing down. But look at the thousands of people with e-commerce stores online. People are doing business on Amazon FBA and Shopify. There are more people doing retail now than there were when all the brick and mortar shops were still open. So there is no retail apocalypse online.

E-commerce is where it is at today, that's where all the growth is coming from. E-commerce is growing year after year. New markets are opening up, and it keeps snowballing. Fast moving consumer goods products are selling online. These are a traditional brick and mortar industry. Online is still small compared to off-line. Much of the online industry is accelerating. There is still a lot of potential with new technologies that will emerge.

It's a mistake to see Amazon as a single monolithic business. The same goes for eBay. Both of these businesses rely upon hundreds of thousands of individual entrepreneurs. So Amazon is like a giant mall full of independent retailers.

The number of people prepared to buy packaged goods online is increasing. It used to be the consumers shied away, apprehensive but now they will buy online. There are still barriers and challenges for consumers doing business online. These need resolution. Some marketers being unscrupulous cause problems. Manufacturers and retailers have to meet the needs of consumers. To increase their willingness to buy online.

Consumer brands are meeting the demand of online shoppers. By meeting their needs, you can capitalize on the growth in the market. Most retailers think as in channels. They organize their marketing teams within the channels. Amazon is itself divided into many channels. Consumers are more multifaceted. They want choice and flexibility, and consumers now like to scrutinize the marketplace. They like to consider what's available before actually making the sale decision. All aspects of the product come into play. From appearance and function to the actual delivery conditions. The consumer will take all these things into consideration.

It's risky for marketers to view things in a traditional way. When there is huge growth things are happening at a rapid pace. Growth is not only from the same consumers or channels that it was before. Marketers need a bird's eye view of the total performance of their activities. Not one retailer but all retailers, not only one channel but all.

The data needs to be complete, accurate and comparable. The method is crucial to the accuracy of data online. By having a bird's eye view, you can pick channels from a different angle. Marketers want visibility of consumers. They want to see how their brand is being interacted with. Knowing the size of the market and its growth rate isn't enough, you have to know in real-time how to perform today.

Speed and simplicity are essential online. There is a vast amount of data but the analytics to derive knowledge from it have to keep up. There are a lot of emerging players who have new operations and processes. It takes forecasting and modeling to match the innovation rate.

It's a cycle of testing, learning and failing in marketing. and technology allows you to speed that cycle up. Consumers don't care about channels they only care about the things they want to buy. If we can look at the total market and get the full picture, that's going to lead to better forecasting models. The specific demand for your brand is going to be in certain places. If you can see that you can assess the whole market and understand how to grow. It takes a big picture, not individual companies measuring their little piece of the pie.

Somehow we have to connect all the marketing data to get an accurate picture. A connected system that talks between segments. This can give an integrated view of the market which will provide better data analytics. This should provide the best commercial opportunity for retailers. Once you have the right tools and partners, it comes down to execution.

Digital data analytics is something new to brick and mortar retail. This can allow you to improve your performance every day by providing a scorecard. You have to know if you're winning or losing, and how to define success. Every brand needs to understand how to define success.

Data, analytics, and execution can work together in a closed-loop. This gives you an understanding. Feedback on your performance, and it can provide sales measurement. You may want to look at your total e-commerce sales in proportion to your other brick and mortar sales. You may want to search across all retail channels at a deep and subtle level. Look at performance with new data which you can measure. You also want to know what the effect of the online market is on your off-line business.

This can give you a clear picture of how you need to move to improve growth. It gives you an idea of the causes and drivers in near real-time which you can then manipulate and influence. Amazon and Nielsen provide consumer data. Some online channels don't provide data or models for measuring performance. New methodologies emerge to overcome that problem.

New analytics companies pop-up, giving new avenues for data collection. Many of the online channels provide segmented data on sales and performance. Facebook, Shopify, all these companies have a broad umbrella of dataflow. You as a consumer of their services only have limited access to that data. They do have the overview that you want. the challenge is access.

Once you have the data that you need, it's essential to move on it. You need to focus, on the demographics and markets and on the actual activities that yield the best ROI.

Analytics are often geared to help you make decisions about your performance. You need to decide a level of alignment and consensus. Before performing your data analytics.

E-commerce is strategic, and you have to be agile as things happen fast online. Increasing the number of data sources improves market visibility for your enterprise. Its about quality of overview.

Expanding brand awareness is the most important thing for marketing executives. Developing customer relationships and brand positioning are also meaningful. The marketing role itself has increased in importance in business. Marketing executives are becoming more cross-functional in their organizations. They have to deal with business strategy, commercial impact, and brand vision. There is an interplay between business strategy and brand vision.

To raise brand awareness, you must first measure brand awareness. If you're not one of the top brands in your vertical then you're not going to be getting the sales. You're not going to be making the conversion now or in the future. How would you define brand awareness? How do you quantify it?

You want to measure it and to grow it. Online, measuring brand awareness is a complicated concept. According to Gartner, 9% of marketing budgets are towards analytics tools. Which is the most of any marketing function. Companies put a lot of money into analytics. Brand awareness isn't the only thing you need to do with your analytics budget. Is measuring social media adequate as a measure of brand awareness? No. It's quite often sacrificed as a consequence.

Much market research on brand awareness is with surveys and psychological questionnaires. This is not practical online from your datasets. There needs to be a better way to measure brand awareness from the available data. Somehow extrapolate it. You can survey 150,000 people to get an accurate picture of brand awareness, but do you want to do that?

Influence is the key. Social media can give us data on influence. But then the question again is how do we measure influence? Influence and brand awareness interrelate, but it's not a complete metric. If you are prevailing on social media, it may give some data on your branding. Social media metrics are relevant and do provide intelligence on brand value. The question is, what is an effective means to measure that brand value in dollar terms?

Can the value of the brand quantify in rating scales? The whole point is a research tool for measuring the value of individual features of a product. It uses real-life data and statistical techniques to model market decisions. Again this technique relies upon surveys. This is a perfect approach for brand measurement. You can alter the features and pricing and those of your competitors.

Conjoint analysis helps to determine how people value different attributes. That make up a product. It's often used to create models that estimate market share. Revenue, and profitability of new products. It can apply to measuring brand equity also.

The bottom line of measuring marketing success is the return on investment. You want to look at that and customer satisfaction when measuring your brand.

CHAPTER TEN

PRODUCT BRANDING CASE STUDIES

SELLING ON AMAZON

Many years ago I took part in a market research focused for a new Gillette product that had not yet released. This was 20 years ago and I forget the name of the razor now but it was very modern and fancy. Nothing like anything that was on the market at that time. They showed us all the TV commercials. Slogans, packaging and the promotional material. We had all signed a nondisclosure agreement and they even gave us a free razor. Which we couldn't get replacement blades for because it wasn't in the stores yet.

One very successful campaign Gillette had was the best a man can get campaign, I'm sure many of us remember that one. So Gillette is a strong brand with a very targeted market that it connects to very well. They don't only sell razors. They sell body wash and shaving foam all sorts of stuff. One of the best ways for them to increase sales is not only to get new customers. It's actually to sell more blades to customers they have.

Yes as weird as it may sound that means encouraging people to shave things other than their face. They market chest shaving and shaving for sensitive areas. So how does

Gillette unify its brand message with this stuff? On top of the traditional shaving market.

Gillette's brand builds from the customer and the customer's mentality. The best a man can get, it's inspirational and they had that nifty song on the advert to go with it.

"You know the feeling, every guy's had it. You're unbeatable, unstoppable. You got that walking-on-water feeling. You look, they smile. You win, they go home. It's the feeling you get every day with the world's best shave. M3 power. Every move is smooth, every word is cool. I never want to lose that feeling."

It's all about the feeling, confidence and self-esteem. Its great marketing and the branding captures the consumer's emotions and passions. Great brands tap into a deeper motion. That gets triggered whenever the consumer contacts the brand.

So Gillette is a great example of a strong brand. Another very strong brand is Amazon. Amazon is itself positioned as a huge umbrella. Below which are thousands upon thousands of brands being marketed and sold. Many of them by large manufacturers and distribution firms. There are many thousands of small entrepreneurs branding products on Amazon.

Many people selling products on Amazon will tell you. The branding and visual presentation are a significant part of their success. Its a growth strategy. Selling on Amazon you're using the same branding principles as you do in the off-line world. So I want to outline the process of branding an Amazon product and give you some tips.

You need to create a unique branding experience for the consumer. That includes differentiation. In the products and in you as the seller, consider what you are offering that makes you unique. It requires a bit of imagination and creativity. Come up with what makes your business unique and different from the competitors. Branding is only one aspect of the Amazon marketing enterprise. You still have to keep working on other important things in your business. Things like building business channels and adding more quality products.

Consumers should see variety in your store when they come to visit. They should be aware that it will be a quality experience. Keep striving for excellence as the consumers on Amazon are expecting exactly that. You have to keep improving to gain a competitive edge. Impressing your customers with new branded product offerings.

The mistake many new sellers make to Amazon FBA is to copy the other successful sellers. Many have been on there for years. If you're doing that will lose out. You have to come out with something new. The products you're selling and the experience of customer service.

You need to come up with a list of product ideas. Do advanced product research and do an ROI analysis. Choose the products that look good and start contacting potential suppliers and manufacturers. Get some samples and look at the design specifications. You need to make it stand out against the competition. When branding on Amazon you have to look at packaging. The brand registry. Also other things including taxes.

Amazon is a great place to experiment with product branding. I always like to contact my suppliers after I've ordered and get a tracking number. It's also a good idea to talk to them about what packaging options are available. If you can have inserts with promotional material. Because this is drop shipping that we are doing even if we are using FBA. You can size these suppliers up and determine if they are responsive or not. Do they speak good English for a start and do they communicate well.

This is an international business so you need to know when they are on line. Generally your start off with messages and if necessary you can chat on the phone. Later if you need to change the product you may want to do a video phone call. You're going to be dealing with the suppliers a lot and it's important to know how to handle them.

The messaging systems on some of the sites like Aliexpress or Alibaba are not up to the job. It takes too long to communicate. You can use chat or Skype messager which are more responsive. It's also a good idea to know what you need to talk to them about first. Make a list of questions that you need answered and asked them one question at a time. It can be confusing for someone that doesn't have English as a first language. Don't ask a stream of questions all at once.

You will need to find a perfect brand name. There will be photography and packaging design. There are also legal requirements to fulfil. There are barcodes and other things that need to job packaging, may be you want a QR code. You may not even know what that Amazon brand registry is. Do you need a trademark?

Product branding on Amazon all these things. When it comes to thinking up brand names in relation to products. If you're stuck, try sticking that product name into Google image search. For example if you are looking up sleeping bags. Stick it into the Google image search and you might see people all snuggled up warm and comfortable. You might see some people snuggled up by a fire. So you can put that term warming comfortable into Google image search and see what comes up. This can trigger some ideas for you it's kind of a brainstorming shortcut.

Don't get stuck on it as it's not that big of a deal if you're going to be bringing out a lot of products. There is no perfect brand name. Another thing is domain availability. You may come up with a great brand name and decide to make a website for the product line. So you want to make sure that the domain name is available. I recently came up with the brand and when I checked for the domain it was available but it was $3000 not the usual 15 bucks. So for that particular brand I've chosen the .biz.

You don't want to use .biz you want to use .com. If it's not available at all may be you should find another brand because at this stage you don't have trademark. Next up you need to find designers and the options are places like fiverr, 99designs and upwork. There are many more places to find designers. Including warrior forum and a bunch of designer websites. Generally I would say 99designs will offer you the best quality at the cheapest price. Fiverr is cheaper still but less on the quality side, I don't hesitate to use it.

99 designs you can run contests and lots of people will submit a design then you choose the best one. You can also put your project up and people will bid to design it for you.

So finding an actual designer is no problem. Generally the communications on the sites a very good and your money is secure too. Generally these sites are places for wheeling and dealing. People like to negotiate prices so don't be afraid to keep your prices down, if you want to haggle you can. There is no need to pay top dollar to get quality. Some people don't go by that ethos though and will fork out the big money.

You need to know how to brief a designer so they can deliver what you want. They will be designing your logo and your packaging. For a logo you're only looking at five or ten dollars. This gives you something good enough to use on an

Amazon product. The good designers will charge a premium rate so ask yourself. If that's what you need then go ahead. 99designs is more a crowd source design. On there you're looking at $300 or more. For that you are getting to choose from many different designs. That's why the quality is better. Big firms spend tens of thousands on logo design.

If you want to get some ideas about packaging you will have to buy some of your competitor's products. Have a look at the real thing. You need to meet Amazon's packaging guidelines at least. There may be safety warnings and other things involved. Take a look at the information they have on the packaging, and what kind of packaging it is. As it a box or a bag, these days' people are very conscious about plastic bags. Take a look at the established brands and how they do their packaging. Are there any requirements for certifications and that kind of thing? For anything electronic there will be.

It's not about what you like or don't like it's about the consumer and what's best for them. Think about the consumer. If it's a camping product you will want to know how much it weighs. If it's a sleeping bag they need to know the temperature range as well. What languages does this information need to be in? If you're in Europe it will need to be in many languages. How about barcodes, QR codes and SKU numbers? You need to have the brand on your packaging as that's one of the requirements of the brand registry.

If there are any other certificates or anything else now is the time to figure out what goes on the packaging. Anything to do of the FDA, or any stamps, certifications and anything like that. Some things are not required by law. Also they are not required by Amazon but still look good to the customer and make it look like a high-end product.

If you have a website you can put your domain on there. At least a contact email address or your support contact details. The packaging requirements are country specific. So keep in mind if you're selling to many markets. Your branding in this respect will need to differ for each segment. Sources of information on packaging include the postal department, courier and delivery firms. Amazon itself and your supplier or manufacturer. They will know about the packaging requirements.

Have a good chat with the manufacturer. What are their different packaging options? Can they do boxes? What kind of bags do they have? Can they put promotional inserts in with the product? There are also inspection companies that inspect products and you can ask them as well. Amazon also has its own restrictions on packaging. The only barcode Amazon generally cares about is that FN SKU. That's the unique identifier for Amazon products. They do also have safety stickers for suffocation and other things.

Your packaging needs to be durable and tough enough for its particular application. You don't want people at the warehouse damaging stuff. Amazon also has rules for this. There is a thing called a GTIN, that's a global trade identification number. There are also UPC and EAN numbers. That FN SKU ticket needs to go on your product. It's expensive to add the UPC and EAN. You can get them from cheap suppliers but should not as it may damage your brand.

You always have to follow Amazon's terms of service. The cheaper route does break Amazon's TOS. Brand registry is where you can register with Amazon that you are the owner of a particular brand. You don't need to do it. It can be an afterthought. Brand registry provides some added protection for your brand and products. There are some extra benefits only available for people on brand registry. It gives you a few more marketing options and protection. The downside is that you need a registered trademark to get it. Registering and trademark takes a bit of time. You can still brand a product and sell it on Amazon without a registered trademark.

You can use one registered trademark to access brand registry. Use this for all your branded products. But then you lose all the legal protection that a trademark is so it's a hack. It may be you don't care about legal protection. Then you can use that trick to access the brand registry on Amazon. Be aware that these tricks that you can learn and use soon add up. You can end up with your whole business being a bunch of tricks which you don't want.

Your trademark doesn't need to be the same as your seller store or your incorporation. They are three different things. It's costly to get a different trademark for each of your brand names. It would mean you needed to file for a trademark each time you launched and tested a new product. Which is of course absurd. You're private-label seller. You want to be adding in testing new products in a streamlined manner. You don't want to be buying trademarks for every single one.

Trademarks can take several weeks to process so do your research first. There is a public database of trademarks where you can look them up in the US and UK. You can be trademark pretty much anywhere in the world and get it into the Amazon brand registry. If you want to sell and the UK or Europe then you need a European trademark. It may be faster to register your trademark in the EU than the US. Then you can get access to the Amazon brand registry that. There's another hack for you.

I won't go into that too much here because Amazon changes the rules. Okay so I guess from this you can see that applied branding is a little different from the theory. Here we are talking about all these rules. Rules for packaging and trademarks. That come into play once the brand development is actually completed. But it's all very much part of the product branding process and its implementation.

Next up is product photographs. On Amazon and with their own e-commerce sites many people make the same mistake. When they are drop shipping they all use the manufacturer supplied photographs. This is a great chance for you to differentiate your branding. Provide high-quality photographs. Have them taken by a professional photographer or by students or yourself. Most of those product photographs on AliExpress end up all over eBay and Amazon and the quality is not high. Many of them don't even have English text on them.

You can order product samples and have your photographs done. You can also have videos which is even better. Many people use their smartphone to do their product photos. As for videos you can do a product unpackaging. If you are redesigning the packaging you want to use that in the video. You can show yourself unwrapping the product. People love to watch that it's like Christmas or birthdays. You can also give a product demonstration. Showing its features and discussing what you like and dislike. This leads into a product review which is also a popular video format. So the videos can be informal and conversational.

That sums it up on the practical side of branding on Amazon.

PRIVATE LABEL COFFEE

Product Branding Marketing

What would you like to have as your own product, with your own name on, that's the concept of private-label. There are a lot of preconceived ideas about private-label. Most people assume that you have to order from China. Rrom AliExpress or Alibaba and that you have to invest a lot of money and pay per click advertising.

You have to do a lot of research and make sure that you have a profitable product. These are some of the preconceived ideas that people have. There's nothing wrong with following the beaten path. Using Chinese products from Ali Baba or AliExpress. But that's not what I want to discuss here. Cost wise of course it's a good option to do that. There are plenty of private-label manufacturers in the United States. Everything from T-shirts, mugs and pens to Christmas ornaments and welding equipment.

There is no shortage of US product. Although it is a little more expensive. Generally it's also of higher quality and of course the shipping is easier. So there are pros and cons. Another abundant niche for products in the US is supplements. But here I'm going to talk to you about coffee or tea. About branding your own coffee brand or how I did it myself. This is a case study on developing your own brand of coffee. I will focus on coffee for the rest of the section. Some people have made millions doing this with tea too.

I'm a big coffee drinker, I like the stuff and talk about it with friends all the time. I'm a big Starbucks girl. It's important to build a community when your branding. It can become a community driven thing. Community is an important marketing tool that's often underused. It's cool if your product can grow out of the community.

There is a lot of scope for building a product for your brand with a community around. If you want to brand coffee then have a coffee community. Where people talk about all the different kinds. People can leave coffee reviews or coffee shop reviews, which would be appropriate.

People can brand and private-label supplements. Then they can do the same with a fast moving consumer good like coffee or tea. There can be a bit of apprehension around food products or nutritional items. Because of regulations. I set about setting up my own brand and I thought about talking to local coffee roasters. There were two or three large ones near by. That was a potential path I could have taken.

To start my research I went to Google and started looking up private-label in my town and in the US in general. I wanted to know if it could work. If I were to repeat the whole exercise I would go with local roasters. But I didn't at the time I looked for US private-label coffee suppliers.

Like I said this can work with coffee and tea. Even with confectionary, chocolate. So many things.

So I found one in particular that stood out for me by the name of paramount coffee. They are in Michigan. I checked out the website and there were a few things that appealed to me about it. I realize looking at the site that I had seen a few of the products in the stores. I like the packaging and they seem to be very ethical. I see they work with rural land and farmers. There is some corporate social responsibility. I like the ethical side of things as that's a potential differentiator for the brand.

They have a lot of manufacturers and they have a private-label program. Different US manufacturers have different private-label programs in the coffee world. Some will do small amounts some won't. These guys do so that was great and quite important. They are also easy to communicate with via email or the phone.

I phoned up and it was all very simple to deal with. They set up an automatic account for me. I asked for advice about private labelling the product. Told them I was branding to sell on Facebook and on my website. I asked about small orders and costs involved. I told them I had a logo and a designer and that I wanted ground coffee.

They sent me a help guide with information on the private-label program. This included info on all their specialty coffee. This gave me a chance to find something that fitted well with my brand as I wanted an organic fair trade coffee. I determined the breakfast blend was the way to go for my market. It fitted and of the whole idea of getting up early and going to work and for my specific market I could tweak it further.

There are opportunities for all kinds of branding. Among their entire specialty blends range. Some of which would make great gifts. The private-label program has a smallest order of 72 bags at 12 ounces or 80 at 10 ounces. I went with the 10 ounce bags which I could sell at a premium. This whole exercise was an experiment in branding for me.

We came up with a color scheme for the branding, and they said that they could do the labels for all we could apply our own. They also gave me a price list. The fair trade organic that I had decided upon was the most expensive. It was around seven dollars a bag. They were not worried about me selling it on Amazon. Some manufacturers are apprehensive about customers selling on Amazon or eBay. In case they also sell on there I made sure to ask them about that first.

They were pretty good in answering my questions about taxes and that kind of thing. Insurance - they take responsibility until it leaves the warehouse. So they are responsible as the manufacturer. You don't need to get manufacturing insurance. Selling on Amazon you may need to ask them about insurance from their point of view. There is always some risk with selling online. So get your legal advice on insurance and find out if you need any liability cover.

Product liability insurance usually runs at about $500 a year. The point is not to be the manufacturer then you don't have to worry about it. But you want to cut your risks and liabilities. I can't give you legal or financial advice so talk to your lawyer. Food products have to go through the FDA and it is a long and expensive process.

We came up with a design for the labels and we made sure that they with the right size for the packaging. We got a template to make sure. The next thing to look at was our pricing and shipping prices. Sometimes sellers will make all their money on the shipping. Going so far sometimes is to offer the product free still turn a profit on the shipping charge.

I found an angle on my branding to do with an underprivileged community group. And I had a talk with the group and got approval to use their photographs on my packaging. So any sales of my coffee allowed a donation to this community cause. I am planning to interview them and share more about them in my marketing strategy. I sell the coffee for $13.99 and it costs about $2.97 to ship.

My profit margin is small. This was only an exercise or proof of concept to experiment with product branding. If I was doing this with profit as the main aim I would have used a cheaper coffee. I would have targeted a very different more upmarket audience. Yoga mums, and have used much fancier packaging, something like that.

That's always an option in the future now that I have the proof of concept. If I bought a cheaper coffee I could have got it for five dollars and sold it for 14 making a decent profit. For me this was a research activity. To sell this on Amazon I would put it in a bag with a sticker embossed on the back. The cost of the label is about $0.50. It's a good idea for you to do a small project like this first up. Before embarking on a more serious product branding enterprise. You may want to do several smaller product launches first.

I set out to find charities from the start as my strategy. When doing this with a more commercial mindset you will want to maximize your profit margin. Then test pay per click advertising campaigns. So you will need a large advertising budget.

The more you practice product branding the better you will get at it. So I set up a website to sell the coffee from, nothing expensive. I use PayPal on there for people to buy the product. There are plenty of options for merchants, PayPal, stripe and others. By doing several of the smaller launches first you can learn the ins and outs of the business. Also have something to show for it in your product portfolio afterward.

CHAPTER ELEVEN

SUMMARY

Branding is very significant to all people in any industry. Whenever you communicate with any employee customer or client, you're representing the brand. Branding and marketing are tactical. An energetic brand is straightforward and very clear. Like Coca-Cola or Apple, Microsoft or Amazon. Everybody working for the firm is aware of the brand identity. Also their responsibilities in upholding the brand.

You have to make your customers excited to see you and excited to be part of your brand. It can be a small thing like leaving them a small branded gift, or it could be something more. Your brand also has to set you apart from everybody else. Your brand has a persona or personality like a person. You determine the customer demographic first. Then shape your brand persona from that. Using the persona designers can create a style guide of colors and fonts. That makes up part of the brand identity. Upholding the promise is the brand persona which determines the entire brand identity.

CONCLUSION

FINDING AND COMMUNICATING YOUR BRAND

Tania Marie Sheldon

If you own your own business what we discuss here will be applicable. Branding is also very relevant to people in management. Any people that have to communicate with a business. Branding is very significant to all people in any industry. Branding could be what people say about you when you're not in the room. Whenever you communicate with any employee customer or client, you're representing the brand.

If somebody is working for you as a subcontractor or consultant, they are part of your brand. They represent that brand. You have to make sure your brand is powerful and that it reflects through all possible channels. Your company culture is a solid part of your brand.

.There is a difference between branding and marketing. While they are interdependent and essential to each other . It is not always clear, so I want to discuss it with you here. Branding is what makes you unique. So you stand out from competitors and how you communicate your uniqueness. That uniqueness defines your benefits to your customers. Branding influences customers. Also your staff and other companies and business people you deal with. You have to make all these people ambassadors of your brand and enthusiasts and fans of your brand. Marketing has more to do with the techniques used in implementing all those things.

Branding and marketing are tactical. Branding is your Birdseye view and long-term target. Marketing is the nitty-gritty techniques that you use like email and social media.

Your marketing methods should project your Brand. An energetic brand is straightforward and very clear. Like Coca-Cola, Apple, Microsoft or Amazon. We all know who and what they are. What they represent and what we can expect from them. As soon as you see that logo, you know everything that serves as a brand. There's much more to it than selling a product.

McDonald's, for example, sells an entire experience. Kids love to go there and see Ronald McDonald and play on the playground. For them it's a big adventure, Burger King or Wendy's is a more a trip to the burger store. Denny's is different again. These brands present themselves in a different way but all are consistent. This is often referred to as authenticity.

For your brand to be authentic and has to be accurate in how it portrays your company. You have to walk the walk and talk the talk. Your brand may present customer service as being high. Then I don't want to be waiting on the line when I phone support. I don't want to see any contradictions to the brand identity. Everybody working for the firm has to be aware of the brand identity. Including their responsibilities in upholding the brand.

Make sure your company does what you say it does and keep that in public view. You have to make those customers excited to see you and excited to be part of your brand. It can be a small thing like leaving them a small branded gift, or it could be something morel. Often it's about establishing intimacy with the customer. You don't want them to think that you're selling them something, instead that you are a friend in some way. You want to establish a real connection with the customers. Resonate with them as a friend.

You need to do all this is the way to solve your customer's problems. In a friendly way that resonates with them, that they will remember. You then want them to share this pleasant experience with friends and co-workers. Your brand needs to set the highest possible standards. Your brand is an expectation and you are accountable.

Your brand also has to set you apart from everybody else. You need to look at those competitors and look at your customers seeking the pain point. What represents a threat to your customers? You can't please everyone. You have to focus on your target audience and find out what matters to them more than anything else. Find your client's primary problem and then find the solution that you can provide. That solution is your differentiation. It's your unique selling point. You want to be the only company that can provide that particular solution. You are the only company that can give the answer in that specific way. Its called alignment, and it relates to your brand's personality.

Your brand has a persona or personality like a person. Your customers also have a persona. A personality representing the most significant demographic. You determine the customer demographic first. Then shape your brand persona from that. So it's portrayed like a person that can communicate to the customer persona. You know the persona of your brand. Things like design and communication are all linked together. These things have to reflect the persona. This makes the whole branding exercise coherent and cohesive. It makes the brand consistent and adds to its authenticity.

Using the persona designers can create a style guide of colors and fonts. That makes up part of the brand identity. The style guide is stuck to in all media. This is a big part of a strong brand that can't alter under different interpretations. You can think of it as a pyramid with the customer persona at the top like the big shining eye. Reflected in the customer persona is the brand promise. Upholding that promise is the brand persona which determines the entire brand identity. Below that in the pyramid are all the communications channels. Channels by which this identity spreads to customer's, staff and everybody else.

Once you have a logo, you can put it out everywhere. In your signatures and photographs, and all your communications. Your text communications must have the same style and font. The same style signature, the same logo, and the same format. This is all part of the brand identity process. Without this consistency, there is no brand. The brand colors should be exact and precise.

Going back to the customer persona, if you don't get this right your entire brand will be off target. Targeting the wrong brand will be a disaster. Know that persona. Familiarity will build a strong your foundation for communication. Often companies will use focus groups and surveys. The customer persona is also known as the buyer persona or customer avatar. You need to know where they shop where they eat, what they like to read, how they enjoy entertainment. Who they vote for, what they like to do for fun, what makes them happy and what they dislike. This information is available. If you've got it right then, you know what customers aren't for you. You know who the right fit for your brand is.

You have to know your competitions brand and customer avatar. You also have to understand your differentiation. How it may make the buyer avatar different from your brands, if it does it all. What exactly is different about your brand persona and theirs. You have to express why your brand is better than the competition. Find the unique selling points. No matter how trivial, as sometimes its something small that can make the customer most happy.

The right decision for the company should be the right decision for the customer. In this way you maintain brand integrity.

Core values are the fundamental beliefs of your organization. This can frame in a single sentence which you have to define. You need to know the core values of your competitors. Core values enable your employees to make decisions in alignment with the brand. It holds your people accountable. Staff have to note that the decisions they make are the right ones for the company. For the client. They have to know what the core values are. The core values define the expectations of the company. Knowing those expectations is what enables staff to make firm decisions.

When running social media campaigns keep things as simple as possible. Often these campaigns run to extract customer data. It could be email for example, A simple funnel may suffice. You have to make it easy for the customer to give you the information. So surveys and optin forms have to be very understandable and easy to use. It has to be direct and straightforward. The same goes for your logo. Those core values are best summed up in a single sentence.

Keep your message simple and direct. You don't want to be too cluttered. Not all your customers will want to give you feedback and neither will all your staff. Sometimes it takes a board meeting or a brainstorming session. You must draw the information out of people. You want to get feedback every single day if you can. In this way, you can keep improving and coming up with new ideas and new features for your brand identity. Once you find what works stay with it.

You have to communicate your expectations. Don't assume that you know what motivates people, let them have input to help you in leading. The brand ambassadors have to have the opportunity to communicate their ideas. Without compromising the brand in its current form. It comes down to internal communication, messaging for example. Many messaging apps designed for project management keep a permanent log of conversations. You can extract information from this data. You can get a feel for the staff's temperament and attitude. There is no reason why a company can't use messaging to understand customers in the same way. If you understand the conversation you have a stronger grasp on the customer persona.

You also want to reward your staff when they present the brand well. You want to condition them to become ideal brand ambassadors somehow. In the same vein, you want to reward customers for spreading the brand values. You can do this with brand engagement programs.

A good leader does not know it all. They can ask questions and have questions asked of them. You need engaged employees. Committed to the success of your brand.